Goodbye Egypt

A Kingdom Entrepreneur's Guide to
Reclaiming the Marketplace

Books by Otescia R. Johnson

He Cheated: A Woman's Guide to Receiving God's Healing After Adultery

Lessons I Learned in the Divorce

I Am Who I Am… & I'm Finally Cool with Her

He Cheated 2: Special Edition

A Christmas Baby Miracle

A Kingdom Entrepreneur's Guide to Reclaiming the Marketplace

Otescia R. Johnson

Copyright © 2019

All rights reserved—Otescia R. Johnson

No part of this book may be reproduced or transmitted in any form or by any means, graphic, electronic, or mechanical, including photocopying, recording, taping, or by an information storage retrieval system without the written permission of the publisher.

B.O.Y. Publications, Inc.
P.O. Box 1012
Lowell, NC 28098
www.alwaysbetonyourself.com

ISBN: 978-1-7338051-0-0

Cover Design: Casting Crowns Media, LLC
Interior Design: B.O.Y. Enterprises, Inc.
Author Photo: Santoria Harris

Printed in the United States.

Dedication

This book is dedicated to every Kingdom Entrepreneur who needs the reminder that entrepreneurship is more than simply owning a business... it is a response to a divine call.

Acknowledgements

With a grateful heart, I honor my readers and friends who have followed me throughout my writing career. You have consistently followed me across multiple genres and recommended my books to others. Without readers, the life of an author would be profoundly isolating and boring. Thank you!

A special thanks goes to Charita Carthen, the friend I never have to give many details to before she cosigns on whatever energy I'm putting out. I love you for life! Thank you, Ingrid Cruthird, for your years of prayers, laughs, family time, and grand vision. I am grateful God brought our families together. Nadeen Cooper and Shakee Perry, thank you for being the road team and sisters I never realized I needed. Knowing I can call on you whenever there is an assignment brings me peace. I love you ladies, and I am cheering you both on as you continue to unveil your gifts to the world! Deirdre Miller… I know we're family, but I'd love you even if we weren't. I'm so encouraged and inspired by the woman you are. I love you, and I can't wait to see what God does next for you. Patrice Gainey, you are a freaking ROCKSTAR. I love you my sister-cousin!

Melissa Nixon, Roshanda Pratt, and Adrienne Young… thank you, Business Besties, for your prayers, examples, words of encouragement, laughs, and willingness to add a fourth to the group. I love how God assembled this team.

To my parents, brothers, aunts, grandmothers, cousins, uncles, and other family members… thank you for your love, support, life lessons, and encouragement. I appreciate each of you and the role you've played in my life. I am a better woman because of all of you.

To Omari, Eric, Abriah, Janae, Adonis, and Elijah…. Raising you guys was the greatest joy of my life thus far. I always prayed to be able to give you a childhood full of joyous memories. When I think back on our road trips, family game nights, impromptu singing and dancing sessions as I cooked dinner in California, the many things you guys hid from Dad and me to protect each other… my heart smiles and I know we did our jobs. If you don't take anything else away from my life's story, remember this… I sacrificed it all so that I could show you what walking out your destiny really looks like. If you ever need a reminder of the power of prayer, faith, and hard work, I pray you'll think back to the many times you saw the example in your own home. I'll love each of you forever.

To my biggest supporter, best friend, confidant, coach, covering, and lover… Lyndell, I love you more than words will ever be able to express. I am the woman I am today because you were always confident enough to push me. You guide me, teach me, and gently correct me when I'm wrong. Your patience, the way you look out for me, the things you do to protect me even when

I don't know I need protection… those things are priceless. I can't thank God enough for you. When He created you, He had me in mind and vice versa. Thank you for believing in me and pushing me to launch out into the deep. Thank you for listening and conversing with me as this book churned in my spirit. Your input and contribution made it better than I could have imagined. I promise to spend the rest of my days repaying you over and over again for being the secret to my success. I love you.

Table of Contents

Foreword 13

How Did We Get Here? 17

Moses, Egypt, and the Red Sea 25

Understanding Your Dominion 37

Recognize Your Positioning 49

You Are Called to Entrepreneurship.................59

Learn the Power of Heavenly Strategies 73

Increasing Your Trust Walk:...............................87

You are Called to Solve a Problem..................101

Know the Purpose Attached to Your Profits..................111

Assume Your Position:......................................127

About the Author...143

Connect with Otescia...145

Foreword

You are about to read one of the most important books ever written. I say this because I used to be one of those people stuck in the rat race, until Otescia helped me find my way off the hamster wheel. Many people are chained to 9-5 jobs that suck the life out of them daily. You may currently be one of them… one that feels oppressed by a job where you have to ask to take vacation, take a lunch break, or even use the restroom. But those days are numbered, because your day of Exodus is near.

I have watched Otescia lead many people from the land of bondage to the world of business ownership. She understands that God did not create us to work for each other. He gave you a gift that is intended to make room for you, not an employer. God has given you everything you need to live a life of fulfillment, purpose, and prosperity. This book will teach you how to live in that fulfillment, find your purpose, and reap the prosperity that God has in store for you.

Otescia is an excellent teacher and woman of God who will take you by the hand and show you the way to a better life. She once felt miserable working for an employer that didn't take the time to remember her name, and now she is working to make sure that the masses remember God's name through her continuous teaching and speaking endeavors. She is working to make sure God gets the glory for all achievements in her life, as well as in yours. So, get ready to experience many life changing revelations in the pages ahead, because the truths contained herein have the power to set you free!

Lyndell L. Johnson
Author, *Grow Into Success*

Kingdom: the realm in which God's will is fulfilled. (Merriam-Webster)

Entrepreneur: one who organizes, manages, and assumes the risks of a business or enterprise. (Merriam-Webster)

Kingdom Entrepreneur: One who operates in the realm in which God's will is fulfilled while organizing, managing, and assuming the risks of a business or enterprise.

No matter what "they" try to make you believe, as a Kingdom citizen, entrepreneurship is a call to form, manage, and personally benefit from a "for profit" extension of your personal ministry.

— **Otescia R. Johnson**

Chapter 1

How Did We Get Here?

I can recall the day God began to birth this message in me very clearly. I was at my desk working on a devotional for a business planner and prayer journal. I thought the planner/journal would be a great way to help entrepreneurs merge their faith and their business. Little did I know, God was birthing something much deeper, much richer within me.

I formatted this planner/journal to match the way I set my work weeks up. I plan both spiritually and naturally. God is the reason I am an entrepreneur. He gave me the desire to work for myself, then nudged me until I surrendered and said yes. As a result, I continually yield the direction of my business over to Him. As I constructed the planner/journal, God led me to various scriptures to help entrepreneurs remain encouraged as they work on their businesses. It was this crucial process that stirred something within me and ultimately led to a change in the direction of this book.

That day while writing a reflection piece, God spoke to me and said, "Remember the red sea... consider the red sea." Now that didn't make very much sense to me when He spoke it, so I grabbed my Bible and reread the story I'd read so many times. It was at that moment that He illuminated something so powerful to me that I began to weep. I don't mean single tears rolling down my cheeks. I mean deep, soul-stirring absolutely UGLY crying as the years of lessons began to click in place in my mind and spirit. The numerous times I cried out to God for an understanding of why my process in business was so difficult, all began to make sense. The gratitude that poured from my heart made me realize for the first time, I was truly on the right path… the path that had been orchestrated for me by God.

When I finally got myself together enough to talk without breaking down into a blubbering mess of gratitude, I shared the revelation with my husband. He listened with the patient smile he always gives me, then asked, "Are you going to do a video about it?" I paused for a second. The pause was mostly due to the fact that I'd already felt led to do a video but really wanted to get out of it. (I'm being totally transparent here.) The other reason I paused was that I am always amazed by the way God uses my husband to push me into my destiny. That caused another wave of gratitude and I started crying all over again. It was during that second cry that I felt the strongest urge to go live on Facebook and share the revelation God had given me.

I obeyed and shared it exactly how God gave it to me. I didn't wait to make it all pretty and fancy. I didn't worry about not having a product to sell at the end of the

Goodbye Egypt

broadcast. I just obeyed God and went live from my PUBLIC page… not the comfortable group I facilitate in private. This was a word for all Kingdom Entrepreneurs and God had chosen me to share it with them. That particular day the live video only had a few hundred views. I was satisfied because I knew I obeyed God. I thought that was the end… BOY WAS I WRONG!

A couple months later, God led me to commit to 90 days of prayer, fasting, and intentional pursuit of Him. These 90 days would include my birthday, a vacation, Thanksgiving, and Christmas… I asked Him, "Are you sure we can't start after the first of the year?" He replied, "You said you wanted your destiny more than anything else. This will only come through fasting and prayer so that I can break the things off you that have been holding you back." Who can argue or debate that?!?!? I surrendered to God and extended the invitation to my secret group so that we could pray and grow together, and so that I would have accountability partners. We prayed every morning at 5 am regardless of the day of the week or what was going on around us. We carved this special time out to pray and hear from heaven. We each committed to fast as we were led by the Holy Spirit. My own personal fasting meant no meat, coffee, sweets, or indulgence food. I love coffee almost as much as I love life, but as an act of obedience, I was willing to deny my flesh that pleasure so that I could feed my spirit. It was during this time of fasting and prayer that God continued to connect more of the dots for me.

Since the beginning of the year, God had been dealing with me regarding entrepreneurs and speaking prophetically about His desire to work through them and their businesses. I never shared much about it publicly but journaled it and shared within the group when I felt led. During the first week of the fast God gave me the idea for this book. I gave it a different title, but the content was basically the same. The focus is centered on sharing with entrepreneurs the magnitude of the weight of our responsibility and position here in the Earth realm. We aren't small business owners. We are Kingdom Entrepreneurs called to reclaim the marketplace and the airwaves for Jesus! When He gave me the idea, I fleshed out a quick outline and sat it to the side thinking I didn't have the time to write another book right now. I already had one due out and four client books to publish. Ya girl was the epitome of booked AND busy!

God, being who He is, was not concerned about my workload. He made sure I knew so when He caused me to run across the Red Sea video. I listened to it again and heard the Holy Spirit say to me, "Share the video now." I obeyed and shared the message again believing it would get in front of the right people… those who are entrepreneurs and doubting whether or not they are on the right track. Within no time, the video began to spread, and more and more kingdom entrepreneurs were following me, messaging me, and sending me friend requests. I started to see testimonies of those who were on the brink of throwing in the towel but received the encouragement they needed to continue.

Goodbye Egypt

I prayed about it and thanked God for helping us all see and hear Him clearly. I thanked Him for bringing so many of us back into alignment with Him. I was on this spiritual high of gratitude when the Lord stopped me in my tracks again. "This is bigger than a Facebook video. This is the book I told you to write." I went back to the outline I'd fleshed out and reviewed it. As clear as day, God had given me the message that would become the foundation of a book. This book is purposed by God to radically shift the mindset of small business owners who are people of faith so that they would realize they have been called to kingdom entrepreneurship.

Entrepreneurship is not something to do because you don't like working for someone else.

When you are in a relationship with God, everything you are attached to must also be attached to your purpose. We'll never reach our full destiny in God holding on to things that do not feed our passion and our purpose. God gave you the desire to start that business because He desires to use it to be a blessing to you! As you read this book, it is my prayer that God speaks directly to your heart. I may be the person typing the words, but trust me… This is ALL God's work. We know that faith cometh by hearing and hearing by the word of God. (Romans 10:17 KJV) As you read, to have faith for the prophecies to come to pass in your life… to have faith for God to bless your business beyond what you can even ask or think, you NEED the word of God spoken directly to your heart. Having a person to confirm what

God speaks to you in your private time of devotion is nice, but the true embedding of the word down within your spirit happens when you hear for yourself. Keep a journal and pen with you as you read. There are many things the Holy Spirit will share as we journey through this book together. We need to be prepared to capture those things so that we may pray and meditate over them during our personal devotion.

Being a faithful steward over the business God has assigned to you is VITAL! This is not just another opportunity for you to make money, this is an extension of ministry by way of the marketplace. We are called to have dominion over the earth. We are called to be the head and not the tail, to be above and not beneath, to be lenders instead of borrowers. To walk this out, we must have our own revenue streams that provide for the lifestyle we are called to live, a lifestyle of abundance and total obedience to the voice of God. There are those of us who are called to global ministry. If that's you, you'll need access to resources to carry out the call. God knew that before He ever formed you in your mother's womb. This is why He called you into the marketplace, so that He may funnel resources to you to carry out the mission. Remember, you are not just a small business owner, you are a **Kingdom Entrepreneur** radically impacting the marketplace and airwaves for Jesus one contract, client, customer, patient, and/or business deal at a time! We are not dependent upon the world's system. We are called to create a new system that reflects the heart of God in the earth.

Goodbye Egypt

Prophetic Word: We are in the middle of a unique season within the Earth. God is causing a shift to happen that is transferring wealth out of the hands of the wicked and into the hands of the righteous. He is bringing us into proper alignment so that we will be good stewards over all He has predestined for us. He is not transferring this wealth for the sake of people becoming wealthy. God is causing a shift to happen so that we will have the resources to reach the world for Him. The end goal of your success is not for you to brag about your own efforts, it is for you to give glory to your God for the wondrous works He's performed in your life so that your life becomes a witness for a relationship with God. God has referred to this time as the great wealth transfer. Those who are in a position with their businesses will see an influx of clients, customers, and patients. Our businesses will overflow with the influx of revenue and we will see expansion in record numbers. This is all to bring glory back to God and to draw those who are impressed by material things. It is the things that catch their attention, but the love of God that will draw them.

Chapter 2

Moses, Egypt, and the Red Sea

This chapter is important because it is the lesson God gave me that provided all of the revelations I needed to solidify my position in the marketplace once and for all. It is what pushed me to stop looking at what I see and use what He has given me to demand the earth realm to line up with what God has revealed to me in the spirit realm. As I mentioned in the opening chapter, God used my time of writing something completely different to make the last few years of my life begin to make sense. After telling me to "consider the red sea", the Lord took me to the book of Exodus. At the beginning of this pivotal book, we learn that the Egyptians feared the children of Israel because of the rate at which they were growing and the might they possessed. They attacked the children of Israel and took them into bondage. However, even in captivity, the children of Israel continued to grow. It is recorded in Exodus 1:12 that the more they afflicted them, the more they multiplied and grew. It is evident even from the beginning, that the children of

Israel were favored by God. How else can you explain the fact that they grew despite their oppressor's enslavement?

The king of Egypt, threatened by this, ordered the midwives to begin killing all of the sons born to Hebrew women. Even in this, God favored the children of Israel because the midwives feared God and did not do as the king ordered. Pharaoh then called the midwives back to him and asked why they disobeyed. Still fearing God more than they feared the king, the midwives lied and told Pharaoh the Hebrew women were stronger than Egyptian women and were delivering their babies without the help of a midwife. Determined to stop the growing power of the children of Israel, Pharaoh then ordered his people to throw all the male babies into the river.

During this course of time, a daughter of Levi gave birth to a male child. She hid her baby for three months before placing him in the brush of the river. It was in that brush that the daughter of Pharaoh found the baby and had compassion on him. She ordered his own mother to nurse him and even paid her to do so. When the child was stronger, his mother returned him to Pharaoh's daughter who would raise him as her own even though she knew he was a Hebrew child. She named him Moses.

While you may already know the story of Moses' birth and how he came to a member of Pharaoh's family, there are a few keys things to point out here. Not only was Moses supposed to be killed at birth, but he was also supposed to be despised by the very people who loved

Goodbye Egypt

and nurtured him. Later in the text when Moses is used by God to free the children of Israel, he is also going against the very household that spared him from death, loved and nurtured him. There are times when God will call you to do things that go against the one you feel loyal to. Let me give you an example of how this plays out in the employment sector.

For those of us who grew up thinking we were going to build a career and work for a great company before retiring and enjoying our golden years, the idea of entrepreneurship may be scary and even feel a bit disloyal. I experienced this while working for a company that despite a few hiccups, had been very good to me. I had a boss who was a sole proprietor who actually cared about his employees. I'd grown as an individual while working there, yet, I lost all joy in the job. I loathed Mondays and felt absolutely uninspired every day. It was at this time God began to deal with me about writing. I knew all of the statistics said writers don't make very much money and with a large family to look after, I couldn't imagine turning against my job for the hope of success as a writer. It simply made no sense to me. Yet, this is exactly what God called me to do. He was asking me to break ranks with the job that had provided for my family, turn my back on the boss that cared about me, and do something with a group of strangers (all of you) because supposedly the strangers were my REAL TRIBE! Huh? That still sounds ludicrous.

However, just as Moses grew up in the comfort of the Egyptian palace even though he was a Hebrew child, I was called to be a leader in entrepreneurship. I was called to lead people just like you out of the bondage of the stable job and into the promised land. Regardless of how the comfortable the palace (job) maybe, if that's not where you are called to, eventually you'll become discontent and unable to remain there. This is exactly what happened to Moses. When he became a man, something inside of him would not allow him to continue to watch the Egyptians abuse the children of Israel. He was so bothered by it that he killed an Egyptian after seeing him hit a Hebrew man. Moses thought no one saw him, but when he was later confronted by two Hebrew men they called him out as a murderer. When the King of Egypt heard of what Moses had done he set out to kill him, but Moses was able to escape. The King who for all intents and purposes was a grandfather to Moses was going to kill him. Let that sink in for a moment. How does that relate to the employment world?

Have you heard the stories of people who have worked for companies nearly all of their lives only to be terminated for a minor infraction? These are people who thought they were returning the loyalty they received from the company, but the second a mistake is made, they are let go. Even worse, what about people who give their entire lives to companies only to be laid off with little to no notice? These are individuals who have shown themselves loyal to a company without understanding the company can't be loyal in return. At the end of the day, companies exist to make money. Their loyalty to you stops the moment you threaten the livelihood of the company. The King's loyalty to Moses ended the

Goodbye Egypt

moment one of his own was killed. It wasn't just about Moses killing a man. It was about a Hebrew man killing an Egyptian, which if you remember, is exactly what the king always feared. Moses at that moment was a threat to the King's country (company) so he had to be dealt with accordingly. If Moses could tell us his thoughts on the matter, I imagine he'd tell us it was a sobering moment for him to sit by the well in Midian and come to the realization that he'd always be a Hebrew (employee) to the Egyptians (employer), and that when push came to shove, they would always be in two separate classes.

Many years after Moses fled Egypt, the king died and the groanings of the children of Israel came up before the Lord. It was because of those groanings, God used the one man whose life had been marked by favor to go back and free his people. There are many things that happened between the time God gave Moses the direction to go tell Pharaoh to let His people go, and the time Moses actually obeyed. Moses did what most of us do. He made excuses as to why he wasn't the person for the job. He doubted his abilities. He told God he didn't have the clout to make it happen. He questioned who would even listen or believe him. He told God he wasn't eloquent of speech as though God didn't already know that. This is the same thing we do when God calls us to entrepreneurship. We tell Him all of our problems, our fears, and our shortcomings as though He doesn't already know. He knows you're in debt. He knows you lack follow through. He knows you're an introvert who would prefer sitting at home doing nothing rather than speaking in front of people. He knows you're lazy. He knows you have low self-esteem. He knows you lack confidence. He knows all of it… and He still called you! You are still chosen regardless of the number of shortcomings you may have.

Despite every mistake I have ever made, I am still chosen by God to lead kingdom entrepreneurs into their rightful positions of dominion so that together we can reclaim the marketplace and the airwaves for Jesus!

I love the way God responded to Moses' excuses. Every time Moses gave a "but God I can't", God replied with a, "Yes you can!" God was proving through Moses that while his shortcomings were very real, He'd already made provision for each one of them. There was nothing Moses could say that would disqualify him because God had already called and equipped him with everything he needed to be the leader he was called to be. The same is true for us. Lord knows I have tried many times over the years to walk away from leading others to freedom, but each time God has prevented me from throwing my blessing away. My blessing isn't only in my successful businesses, it is in showing other Christians how to get free. The joy that swells in me every time I see someone win in their business is indescribable. Those same people have turned around and blessed me with their testimonies and referrals. That feeds a place inside of me that a job could never fill. It gives me the satisfaction of knowing I am doing exactly what I was created to do. Despite every mistake I have ever made, I

Goodbye Egypt

am still chosen by God to lead kingdom entrepreneurs into their rightful positions of dominion so that together we can reclaim the marketplace and the airwaves for Jesus! The people that I once saw as strangers are now my family. We are one body in Christ moving towards a common goal of showing the world there is a more excellent way to live. We are yielding our lives to God together! The strength from knowing I am not on this journey alone pushes me right to the face of Pharaoh to declare: Let my people go!

When Moses finally made it to Pharaoh, an interesting thing happened. Instead of God softening Pharaoh's heart to make the process easier, God did the opposite. At every turn, God hardened the heart of Pharaoh so that he would refuse to let the children of Israel go. I've often wondered why God would do that. It was hard enough for Moses to answer the call, why would God then intentionally make the process difficult? What God said to me blew my mind, but it made perfect sense. Every excuse Moses gave was valid. He had issues that needed to be dealt with, including small faith. It is recorded that God spoke to Moses through a burning bush which was a miracle by itself, yet Moses still doubted people would believe God had actually sent him. God even showed him a sign by having him throw his rod to the ground and that rod became a serpent which Moses ran from. Yet, at God's direction, Moses grabbed it by the tail causing it to become a rod again. Then God to Moses to stick his hand into his bosom. Moses obeyed and when he pulled his hand out, it was leprous as snow. God told him to put his hand back into his bosom. This time when he pulled it out, the flesh had returned to normal. (Exodus 4:1-7) After all that, Moses still had an issue with doubt. It was because of this doubt… which can be a serious character flaw for believers, that God had to repeatedly harden Pharaoh's heart as He worked on Moses' character and strengthened his faith.

It is often said that people appreciate things more when they have to work for them. If God were to call you off of your job one day and give you a multi-million-dollar business the next, you wouldn't know how to handle it, nor would you appreciate it as much as you do when you work for it. Continuing in the face of adversity is what propels us into deeper appreciation when success manifests. Each time God gave Moses an instruction, He also told him what the result of that instruction would be. For example, in Exodus 10:12 the Lord told Moses to stretch out his hand over the land of Egypt for the locusts, that they may come upon the land all that day. When Moses obeyed and did exactly as God said, the locusts swarmed in from everywhere covering the land and eating up all of the herbs. Such was the case with each plague. As Moses obeyed God, God did exactly what He promised. Through these exercises of faith, not only did Moses' doubt lessen (we know this because Moses began to obey without rebuttal), but God was also increasing the faith of the children of Israel. They had been in bondage so long, that it became the norm for them. Taking them to freedom was going to require a purging of their old mindset and small faith.

Goodbye Egypt

When God calls you out of the world of being an employee, into the kingdom of entrepreneurship, He takes His time to perform miracles to increase your faith and purge you of your 9-5 mindset. In modern-day His miracles often look like Him providing a way for you to pay your mortgage at the last second. It looks like Him walking you through the beginning feast or famine years, holding your hand as you cry after yet another deal falls through. It looks like God allowing you to experience a set back so that He can set you up for radical growth in the future. He's not sending swarms of locusts to increase your faith, He's working through your business every day to prepare you for miracles and opportunities that are beyond your scope of vision right now. He's causing you to learn how to trust Him even when everything around you is saying stay in that comfy job because you know you're going to get a paycheck every two weeks. God is teaching you to trust Him so that He can bring you out of bondage into the promised land!

As Moses continued to walk into obedience, Pharaoh did eventually agree to let the people go, only to later change his mind (after God hardened his heart) and begin to pursue them. As it is written, in Exodus 13:18 God led the people about, through the way of the wilderness of the Red Sea. This means God knew they would be pursued, yet He still led them this way as opposed to leading them through the land of the Philistines where they may have had to go to war. (Exodus 13:17) He knew the Red Sea was there, yet He intentionally led them there, and here's why. The Red Sea was a pivotal moment, not just because it was the turning point in ending the enslavement of the Israelites forever, but because it proves to us that God will never lead us to a place He doesn't already have a solution for. Everything they needed to cross over the Red Sea was already in Moses' hand. All of the miracles and plagues performed before they left Egypt were signs to build their faith so that when faced with the Red Sea they would have confidence in their God to bring them through. Instead, like many of us, they shrunk back in fear and began complaining. They said to Moses, "Did you bring us out here to die because there were no graves in Egypt?" They even reminded him that they never asked to be rescued. In fact, they told him to leave them alone and let them serve the Egyptians. (Exodus 14:10-12) Remember it was their cries that rose before the Lord and caused Him to send Moses to free them, yet when they were presented with an obstacle, they cried to be left alone for they'd rather die in slavery than in the wilderness.

How many times have we cried to God for deliverance from jobs we hate, only to cry for a new job when the path of entrepreneurship becomes difficult. In those critical faith-building moments, when we are presented with the Red Sea, instead of crying to go back to Egypt (a job), we should use the opportunity to stretch out our rod and command the earth to make way for us. You have an opportunity to speak to the seeds you've sown and demand them to produce a harvest. When you exercise your faith by speaking God's word over the opposition you face, you open the door for God to cause the miraculous to happen to you. On the other hand, when you cry out in fear, you limit the movement of God in

Goodbye Egypt

your situation because without faith it is impossible to move God. (Hebrews 11:6)

The children of Israel were moved in fear, their faith wasn't strong enough for the opposition they were facing. If God had made the release process quick, Moses' faith would not have been strong enough to believe for himself and all of them. He would not have had the courage to even stretch out His rod over the Red Sea and believe that God was going to do what He promised. Because God spent time proving Himself to Moses in private, when Moses stood before the people, he stood in full assurance of the abilities of God! They were able to walk across on dry land because of the authority and faith of Moses who had already been on a journey with God before Pharaoh released them.

It's not what we do in front of people that empowers us for this journey. It's what we do behind closed doors when no one is watching. The power and authority come from those years God keeps you hidden, those years it looks like all the work in your business has been in vain. Those are the equivalent of Moses' hand in bosom experiences. No one else was there to see the miracles happen, but they happened nonetheless, and they shaped Moses into the faith-filled leader God has called him to be. That's why the bible teaches us not to despise small beginnings. (Zechariah 4:10) It is through those small beginnings that God shapes us. He purges us of selfish ambition and teaches us to view ourselves the way He sees us. During those hidden moments, Moses was challenged to grow beyond his shortcomings so that He could be prepared for His greater purpose in God.

Who are you intended to lead? Your journey to freedom is not only about you. Just as Moses was called to an increased level of faith for the purpose of leading his people, we are also called to increased levels of faith for the people we are called to lead. Kingdom entrepreneurship is not just about you becoming successful in your industry. It goes far beyond that. You are called to reach people for God. You are called to be an example of what a life lived for God looks like. You are called to make an impact on those who otherwise may never come into the faith. That's why the journey is so difficult. God uses the difficulty of the journey to work out the kinks in your character. He intentionally makes the process hard so that your faith may be strengthened so that when you emerge into public view and begin to lead the people you are assigned to lead, you'll be properly equipped for the journey. You'll have the full understanding that when opposition arises, all you have to do is open your mouth and declare the word of the Lord over the situation. You must understand your hands already hold everything you need to overcome every obstacle you will face! Stretch out your rod Moses! Stretch out your rod!!!

Chapter 3

Understanding Your Dominion

One of the greatest reasons the children of Israel were so comfortable in bondage is because they did not understand they had been called to dominion. A person who does not know they are entitled to freedom will settle into a rhythm of enslavement, adopting a lifestyle of limitations as "everyday life". The bible is very clear on God's stance concerning the dominion of man. Genesis 1:26 states:

"And God said, Let us make man in our image, after our likeness: and let them have dominion over the fish of the sea, and over the fowl of the air, and over the cattle, and over all the earth, and over every creeping thing that creepeth upon the earth."

Not only did God fashion mankind after His own image, but He gave an immediate decree for him to have dominion, not just over the animals that inhabit the Earth, but over ALL the Earth. Being given such power by the

Creator means we came into this Earth with the authority to command the Earth to line up with God's word.

According to Merriam-Webster dictionary, the word dominion is defined as law; supreme authority; sovereignty. If we were to go back to our elementary school days and use this word in a sentence, we could say, "God has given man supreme authority over all the Earth." Think about that for a moment, the Creator of all things chose a man as the His highest form of creation, giving us supreme authority over everything else He created! We were created to reign from the very beginning. With that being so, why would we ever leave our seat of dominion and submit to the limited authority of the world around us? The world around man was never intended to dictate man's actions. Man was created to have supreme authority over the Earth. Everything I have been given authority over, I have a God-given right to speak to and set in order.

Merriam-Webster defines sovereignty as freedom from external control. When we use this definition to further understand our dominion, it becomes clear God set man up for a life of freedom from the very beginning. We were never intended to struggle with bondage brought about by another person or any world system.

For a person who has been called to entrepreneurship, working a 9-5 can be torturous bondage, particularly if that 9-5 is not tied to your passion and purpose. I can remember the last few years of my traditional employment. I was miserable nearly every day. Not just at work, but I generally felt discouraged and unfulfilled everywhere I went. The discontentment left me frustrated and caused me to isolate myself emotionally. I found fault in others to avoid facing what was really bothering me. I spent countless hours in prayer trying to identify why I was upset. I had a pretty good paying job doing work that didn't challenge me at all. I had an amazing husband who would move Heaven and Earth to please me. I had healthy children who made me laugh every single day. I had a beautiful home. I was healthy and lived an active lifestyle that included walking 3-6 miles a day surrounded by beautiful scenery. From the outside, I should have been happy, but I wasn't. I wasn't anywhere near happy. In fact, those walks were my attempt to rid myself of daily frustration so that I would not allow my discontentment to settle in my home and affect my husband and children. It took a transparent moment with God for me to realize the root of the issue.

The answer to my problem was an internal process that would free me from external control.

I watched an episode of Oprah's Masterclass about the life of the great Maya Angelou. It was a powerful episode in which the famed orator shared poignant stories of her life. She discussed her childhood and the tragedy that led her to discover the power of her voice. I was moved by her commitment to the people, things, and ideas she felt passionate about. I cried as she gave us a glimpse of the depression she experienced after learning of the death of Malcolm X. I wept even harder when I realized what God was showing me. I was no longer watching a documentary-style television show about a famous poet. God was giving me a glimpse into my true calling, the answer to the deep discontentment that was tightening around me with each passing day. The answer to my problem was an internal process that would free me from external control. For me, freedom was in embracing who He created me to be. Years prior, God had spoken to my heart and told me I was a writer. I accepted this title, but never truly embraced it as a part of my identity. I wore it like a removable outer garment rather than allowing it to permeate my heart and spirit so that my mind could be transformed into what God already created me to be. Through someone else's life, God was showing me what happens when a person knows who they are and walks fully in their destiny. The job felt like bondage because, for me, it was! I am called to be a writer which means I literally create something out of nothing. The written word is the vehicle I use to completely shift the mental perspective of the reader. That is my gift. It is my talent. It is the thing I can do with little to no effort. Right here, behind this desk, typing away as though my very life depends on it… this is my place of freedom. As long as my days were filled trading my time for money, I was forfeiting my ability to experience the freedom I was born to thrive in.

Once I understood I'd never feel fulfilled until I answered the call God placed on my life, I faced a whole new battle. What I knew God was calling me to is a field that is difficult to break into and often pays very little. Most writers supplement their income by working a full-time job. I went back to God with my concern. How was

Goodbye Egypt

I supposed to help my husband provide for our family if writers didn't make enough to live on? His response to me was short. In fact, it was only two words, "Trust me." As you can imagine, those two words did nothing to calm the raging fear within me. This process of me crying out to God and Him replying, "Trust me," lasted much longer than I'd like to admit. Nevertheless, God got through to me and I began focusing on writing and trusting Him to work everything else out. Little did I know, His working everything out would mean Him providing me with the revelation to achieve everything He whispered to me in those quiet moments alone with Him.

Understanding my dominion was one of the key factors to me being able to fully grow into the writer He called me to be. To fully embrace my call, I had to release the anxiety that surrounds earning money. I had to trust God when He said He'd provide for my family. As I stated, this was a process, but each month that passed, God proved Himself to be the ultimate provider. He began taking me to various scriptures to remind me that He was in control of everything that affected me and that He had given me dominion over all that I could see within the earth. Dominion was important because it meant that as a result of the praise I offered to my Heavenly Father, I had the God-given authority to speak to the earth and demand it to yield its increase. (Psalm 67:6)

I didn't have to fear to enter the world of full-time entrepreneurship because I was answering a call. God will never call us to something and then fail to provide for us as we follow Him. (Romans 8:28-30). I didn't randomly decide I wanted to be a writer or follow in the footsteps of Moses and lead people to freedom. I was content doing what I'd always done... until I wasn't. The overwhelming call of God came to rescue me from Egypt just as He rescued the children of Israel. He saw that I had only conditioned myself to believe working for someone else was my destiny. I had been conditioned by the world's system to believe I was supposed to get a good job and stay there until retirement. That was never His design for me. He created me for dominion. Dominating whatever field I am in is not just a personal ambition, it is a spiritual concept. Dominion is a Heavenly principle. How can you ever experience dominion in your field if you are employed by someone else? Your employment efforts are intended to make the company look good... to help the company dominate. That isn't God's design. That is the flawed design of a man who is outside of His rightful seat of dominion.

When faced with the Red Sea, the children of Israel reminded Moses that they'd asked him to allow them to stay and serve the Egyptians. They were so conditioned by their experience of enslavement that they likened it to voluntary servitude. Imagine the condition of a man's mind when he'd rather be a slave than take the risk of being free. It was through years of being beaten down by the Egyptians that the Hebrew people forgot how God favored them. Because their deliverance was delayed, they gave up hope and accepted their positions as slaves as their lot in life. They accepted torture, harsh treatment, and bondage. They grew comfortable in their

Goodbye Egypt

dysfunction because it was at the forefront of their human experience. As the years passed, they forgot they were once a strong, God-favored, flourishing nation of people.

Often, when we are faced with the difficulties of starting and growing a business or ministry we do the same thing. In the moments of frustration, we cry out for deliverance from the job. The second a lay-off or termination happens, and we are faced with financial difficulties, we immediately turn to update our resume and completing job applications. When you do this, you are showing God where your faith lies. You are showing God that even though He heard your cry and answered your prayer, you have more faith in the employment sector than you have in Him. You are proving through your actions that you trust a job as your source and not God. It is a dangerous place to be in when anything is trusted or valued over God. You can confess all day that your faith is in God, but when your innate, immediate response to trials is to turn anywhere except to God, you are proving your faith lies somewhere else. Have you forgotten, oh children of Israel, how faithful God, your God, has been to you? Have you forgotten how favored you are? Have you forgotten how He has caused you to flourish in spite of everything and everyone that has attempted to destroy you? God forbid!

Through our natural experiences here in the Earth we have been conditioned to believe a job is a key to our success when God is trying to remove us from the limitations of someone else determining what our time is worth. True success comes from following God all the way through the wilderness into the Promised Land. It comes from allowing Him to build our faith and expand our capacity to receive from Him so that we are prepared to enter a lifestyle of more than enough. God can't elevate you beyond your faith. The time in the wilderness, the time of transition between employee and thriving Kingdom Entrepreneur is intended to transform the way you view yourself as well as your position in the Earth.

Do you know what really stopped the children of Israel from entering into the Promised Land? It wasn't their complaining as most suppose. It was their inability to grow in their trust in God enough to believe the Promised Land was their destiny. They couldn't shake the years of bondage and the mental strongholds associated with it. Though they were a freed people receiving manna from Heaven daily, they simply could not believe they were going to inhabit a place of freedom every day. They were stuck in survival mode, unable to shift to a place of faith for more than enough. The daily manna was okay because it didn't require them to believe beyond their current reality. The promised land meant believing God to take them to a place of more than enough. They couldn't trust God enough to take them beyond their current perspective. They died in the wilderness because He couldn't take them past their place of belief.

Why do you think so many believers before us have died broke and broken? God is faithful. His promises are recorded all throughout the bible. The flaw was never with

Goodbye Egypt

God. It is and always was within our thought process and lack of faith. If you can't believe God will provide for you, you'll tie His hands. Your faith and capacity to receive from Him are the prerequisites of your breakthrough. Just as a college student must take College Algebra I before they are allowed to take College Algebra II, we must have the faith and capacity to receive the fullness of the promise before it will manifest. God is intentionally leading you to the promised land (entrepreneurship) through the way of the wilderness of the Red Sea. (Exodus 13:18) He is using this time to teach you about His promises for you. He is elevating your faith by proving Himself to be a faithful provider. He is purging you of the familiarity of enslavement because you can't be an enslaved man and a free man at the same time.

Romans 12:2- And be not conformed to this world; but be ye transformed by the renewing of your mind, that ye may prove what is that good, and acceptable, and perfect, will of God.

This scripture is often quoted to admonish us from the sins presented to us by the world. I want you to apply it to the way we have been conditioned to believe employment for someone else is the only pathway to success. Be not conformed to this world… Do not accept the traditional lifestyle of subservience as the will of God for your life. Just as the children of Israel became comfortable in slavery, many Christians are stuck in the comforts (salary, benefits) of a job that does not assist them in fulfilling the will of God for their lives. Our instruction is clear. BE NOT CONFORMED! Instead, be ye transformed by the renewing of your mind. To be transformed means to be changed. God wants you to be transformed. He doesn't want you to change to another job, change industries, or even change cities in a thinly veiled attempt to find satisfaction. God wants Y-O-U to be literally changed by the renewing of your mind! To renew your mind means to literally bring your mind into alignment with the word of God. This is done through intentional time spent in His presence, prayer, fasting, and reading His written word. It is through this time with Him that your heart and mind come into alignment with His heart and mind. Over time our thoughts and decision making are no longer fashioned after what we see in this world, but they are patterned after the heart of the Father. It is through this method of being changed by the renewing of our minds that we are able to prove what is that good, acceptable, and perfect, will of God. Here's a hint: His will is that we live in abundance. (John 10:10)

In order to prove the will of God in our lives, we must submit our minds to Him that He may purge us of the world's mindset and embrace the freedom He has for us. This is not a call to live in excess for the sake of excess. That is not God's will for us. His call to kingdom entrepreneurship is a journey intended to bring us back to our rightful place of dominion. I must also point out that everyone will not be called to dominion in the same manner. For us, it is through entrepreneurship, for others, it may be through ministry or work in other areas. However, make no mistake, every man and woman that walks the face of the Earth is called to dominion. In

Goodbye Egypt

order to receive that dominion, God is preparing you and me by leading us through the wilderness by way of the Red Sea. It will be difficult. You will want to quit. There will be years of plenty. There will be seasons of famine that require you to trust God for every provision in your life. There is no way around this because just like the children of Israel, God must prepare us before we can enter. He must bring us into proper alignment with Him. It is our job to learn from the mistakes of the children of Israel. Their lack of faith, the fact that they didn't allow God to changed them through the renewing of their minds, kept them from ever stepping foot in the promised land.

Generations of believers who came before us made the same mistake. They died waiting on the promises of God because they waited on the surface but fainted in their faith every time they faced a Red Sea moment. Their lack of belief tied the hand of God and held up their blessings. Even though it is God's will that you live in abundance, He won't overstep your will to get you there. You must yield your perceptions, pre-conceived notions, and world-inspired ambitions to Him. Offer the things you have become accustomed to back to Him, so that He may replace them with the things He has planned for you. You were created for dominion. Trust Him to lead you through the wilderness and into the promised land where success and dominion are your portions!

Promise Activation: In this chapter, we discussed your dominion and God-given right to freedom and abundance. Now, let's stretch our faith and make a declaration concerning our businesses. Psalm 67 teaches us that we must praise God in order for the Earth to yield her increase. After you make your declaration (speak to the Earth realm and demand it to come into alignment with Heaven), be sure to give praises to God to activate His promises and cause the Earth realm to begin to offer up what is rightfully yours!

I decree and declare that I am a kingdom entrepreneur. God uses my business as an avenue to bring finances and resources to me and my family. Every client, patient, partner, or customer that patronizes my business is blessed because they are sowing into good ground. They reap a harvest as a result of working with me. My cupboards are perpetually filled, and my revenue continues to grow year after year. Every promise God has spoken over my life and business is manifesting now. I speak to the winds of financial increase and command them to blow in my direction. I speak to the rain of abundance and declare it to rain down on me now. My business is growing at God's perfected rate of expansion, and every deal I enter into works out in my favor. I bring a blessing into every room I enter, and corporations are lining up to work with me. I am sought after for my industry knowledge and favored amongst my peers. I am the righteousness of God and success is my portion! The Earth realm is beginning to yield her increase to me even now. In Jesus' name, Amen!

Chapter 4

Recognize Your Positioning

During the early years of my walk with God, I struggled with maintaining my faith during times of intense adversity. I would cry out to God to help me hold on until He delivered me. This would be my go-to prayer every single time the road became rough. I literally had no other verbiage. I didn't ask for strength. I didn't ask Him to speed up the process. I only asked for help in holding on. As a result of my request and my faith level, God helped me to hold on and remain committed to Him until the storms passed. As I grew in my relationship with Him, my wisdom and understanding grew. My prayers began to change from "help me hold on" to show me what needs to happen in order for this to pass. What lesson am I supposed to learn from this? Once God gave me revelation on the matter, I'd thank Him for teaching me, repent if necessary, and then ask Him if we could move on. From that day to this one, I still maintain this type of communication with God. I thank Him for revealing the lesson. I ask Him to help it remain at the forefront of my mind. I repent and ask anyone else I may have unknowingly wronged to forgive me, and I ask God, "Can we move on?" There is no theatrics, no laboring in prayer for days or weeks, no beating myself up. I moved from emotional responses to the understanding I have been positioned in a place with God that allows for me to ask questions, seek His guidance, and ask for the promotion. That is my right as His daughter. I do not go to Him in fear or shame. He saw everything I would do before He ever formed me in my mother's womb, but He still chose me and equipped me for this journey. I am a prepared person, on a prepared path to destiny! I do not give up. I do not wallow in doubt or self-flagellation. I ask my Daddy to basically "get to the point" so that we can move forward in the things He has called me to. After all, this is a relationship and I speak freely with those I am in a relationship with. God already knows how I feel about long, dramatic, over the top conversations about the same topic over and over again, so why would I hide that from Him? I am a "get to the point" kind of girl, and He allows me to be myself. Understanding that I have the right to this relationship with God… this position of sonship… this freedom to be completely naked before Him, expressing my every thought from a place of total transparency… THIS is what opened me up to the ability to recognize my positioning.

This process began with me understanding God's correction towards me wasn't because I was so terrible and sinful. It wasn't because I was constantly messing up and missing the mark. It wasn't because I was somehow unworthy of the call He placed on my life. God corrects me because He loves me and has engrafted me into the fold as His child.

Hebrews 12:6-7 – For whom the Lord loveth He chasteneth, and scourgeth every son whom He receiveth. If ye endure chastening, God deals with you as with sons; for what son is he whom the father chasteneth not?

Understanding this scripture brought me so much peace about my relationship with God and my position within the Body of Christ. I am corrected because I am His child and He wants the best for me. I stopped saying that I was unworthy of the call He placed on my life, or unworthy of the blessings He's prepared for me. Just as I love blessing my natural children and seeing the excitement in their eyes, God sees me the same way. The rough moments in my life come to bring correction so that I can grow in Him and be able to handle the gifts and blessings He has for me. I am corrected because I am loved! Now that I know that, I eagerly ask Him for revelation so that we can move beyond the lesson and on to the next level.

Another key factor in understanding my positioning happened when I realized I didn't have to work to receive promises. I grew up in God believing I had to work to be worthy. I thought I had to serve in every area of the church I possibly could. I thought those works would somehow cancel out the sins I committed. Understanding the power of the cross totally changed my perspective from one of work to one of acceptance. When Christ went to Calvary and shed His blood for the remission of my sins, He made me worthy. I am not called to work my way into heaven or into God's grace and favor. I'm called to accept the access that has already been granted to me. Our walk with God is about understanding the work to redeem man has already been completed, therefore, we have been adopted into the household of faith. Thankfully God doesn't adopt us as sons only to later reject us, He brings us in permanently through the blood covenant of the crucifixion of Jesus Christ.

When Moses grew into a man, Pharaoh, who'd previously accepted him, rejected the fullness of who he was. Once Moses took the first step towards becoming the leader of his people, Pharaoh no longer saw Moses as a member of his family. This happens with us when God begins to shift us from children of the world to joint heirs with Christ. Those around us may not understand our calling or even accept that we have a higher purpose beyond what they can see. It can be one of the most painful experiences to have to walk away from relationships that are no longer serving us or to accept that God has called us to positions of authority in Him that don't allow certain behaviors.

As you are called to kingdom entrepreneurship you will be judged by those who do not understand what God is doing through you. There will be naysayers, possibly within your close circle of friends and family members, who will tell you to remain in Egypt… to basically ignore what you know is right. They will talk to you about the economy and what is happening in the world. They will

Goodbye Egypt

warn you about the number of businesses and ministries that fail. They will suggest stepping out on faith is irresponsible because you have a family to provide for. There will be subtle hints, overt statements, and downright rude comments. When those moments arise, remember God is giving you an opportunity to learn a lesson. Don't fall into the trap of offense. Do not allow rejection to take root within you. Ask God for the lesson He is revealing to you and remind yourself you are no longer of the world, but you have been adopted as a child of God! Those who are not of this spiritual covenant are not equipped to understand this journey because they have not been called to it.

You cannot be free and bound at the same time.

Just as it was with Moses, those you love, those who previously supported you may turn their backs on you. In those moments when the pain grips your heart, it is imperative that you focus on the positioning you have been called to. Moses was called to lead the Israelites. He couldn't do that and remain in Egypt at the same time. If he wouldn't have separated himself from the palace, he would have never been able to walk in the fullness of his calling. So many times, we try to walk in the new while holding on the old. It's impossible. You can't access the promised land while holding on to the place of bondage. Again… you cannot be free and bound at the same time.

When God calls you into kingdom entrepreneurship, He calls you away from everything and everyone that prevents you from answering the call. You may remain cordial, but you can't stay in covenant with the world and embrace covenant with Jesus at the same time. There is a choice that you must make. Will you assume the new position you have been called to, or will you allow the pain of separation from the old hold you hostage?

As you make the decision to embrace your new position you must understand that God is not separating you to cause you pain. He is teaching you lessons to mature you so that you will be equipped to properly steward the authority that accompanies your new position.

Ephesians 2: 4-6 But God, who is rich in mercy, for his great love wherewith he loved us, even when we were dead in sins, hath quickened us together with Christ, (by grace ye are saved); and hath raised us up together, and made us sit together in heavenly places in Christ Jesus.

We have been made to sit together in heavenly place. This elevation is not about being elevated for the sake of being seen or gaining wealth. God never does anything without purpose being attached to it. No, this elevation is about the authority God has given us. Just as your children are given equal authority according to their ability to handle the power that comes with it, God equips His children according to our ability to steward the power and authority attached to His purpose for our lives. As a kingdom entrepreneur, you must be mature enough to walk in integrity when no one is looking. You must be able to follow the voice of God and trust Him even when He does not reveal the full process to you.

Goodbye Egypt

You must be able to hear Him clearly and respond to EVERY direction He gives.

The intense moments of molding you into the person God has called you to be all work together to bring you into the full understanding of your position in Him as well as your position in the marketplace. You are not only called to bring order to your business but as kingdom entrepreneurs, we are called to be leaders in our industries. We are called to establish and keep order because we are to follow after the example our big brother Jesus has set before us. In Matthew 28:19-20, Jesus gives the disciples the instruction to go and teach all the nations to observe everything He has taught them. We typically only reserve this passage for spreading the gospel of Jesus Christ, but God is not that limited. He is concerned with the whole man. He is concerned about how we obtain wealth and what we do with it afterwards. This passage is our proof that we are to share the teaching and revelation God gives us concerning kingdom entrepreneurship and our respective industries. God is not only for the church… He is for everyone, everywhere! With wisdom, we are called to bring order where chaos once reigned.

Think of how the people of the world view the rich and famous. Some idolize them, some are disgusted by them… very few respect them. Yet, these people influence everything from the images we see on television to regulations that impact our financial systems. When people have no confidence in the ones making the decisions, they lose hope for a brighter future. It is the lack of hope that leads people to desperate measures like crime and even suicide. When the Body of Christ assumes our rightful positions here in the Earth realm, we'll gain the influence we need to change the world. God positions us for wealth and greatness not just so that we can be rich and powerful, He gives us this position so that we can bring order and point humanity back to Him.

Your call to entrepreneurship is so much deeper than you just owning a business. God intends to use this call to right many wrongs within the Earth. He has watched man violate His ordinances and establish their own laws. He has witnessed the fall of humanity over and over again. Yet, just as He responded to the cry of the children of Israel when the Egyptians became hard taskmasters, God is responding to the cry of the remnant of believers who desperately want to see Him reflected in the Earth at the highest levels of visibility. He isn't responding with Moses this time... He's responding with you! You are the answer to someone's prayer! You are being positioned to introduce someone to freedom from the things that held them down.

In Daniel the 10th chapter, Daniel gives us a beautiful illustration of how prayers are answered. He begins the chapter by giving us a very powerful statement: "...The thing was true, but the appointed time was long." It seems the people of God have been waiting for deliverance from the corrupt systems of injustice and greed for many years, but God's message of salvation and deliverance are true! We were only waiting for the appointed time. I truly believe we are seeing a time and season upon

Goodbye Egypt

the Earth that has never been seen before. Just as God sent the answer to Daniel's prayer the moment he spoke it, God sent you the moment the people prayed. Yet, the enemy attacked the messenger angel before he was able to deliver Daniel's answer to him. God then sent reinforcements in the form of the Archangel Michael to assist in the fight so that the angel may be released to deliver the answer to Daniel.

While you were experiencing your time in the wilderness, while you were going through rough patches, while you were losing friends and family members, God was preparing you so that the moment you were ready He could send angelic reinforcement to make sure the answer (You) could be released to His people. Your leaving Egypt was the moment the prayer was prayed. Your walking through the wilderness was when the reinforcements began their fight in the heavenlies. The moment you cross into the promised land will be the moment answer meets the people who have been fasting and praying before the Lord for help, strategies, and answers!

God has positioned you as a change agent in the earth.

Your business is purposed to revolutionize your industry. If your mindset is not to dominate globally, consider this your clarion call to action. You are a joint heir with Christ to the throne of God. You are spiritual royalty sent to the Earth to bring order and support the transformation of those you are purposed to help. Your position is one of authority and dominion! When you speak, the world around you MUST obey!

In Genesis, when God spoke to the Earth and told it what to do, everything He spoke to obeyed. He said, "let there be light," and there was light. He didn't ask for light to come upon the Earth. He directed light and light obeyed. This is the eternal bloodline you have been adopted into. You were made in the image and likeness of God. You were commissioned to do greater works than the works Jesus performed while He walked the Earth. How can we know these things, yet still never enter into the promised land? How can we read the mistakes of the children of Israel and still miss the mark? The answer is in the lack of understanding for our positioning! When you don't understand how God has set you up for success and positioned you within the body to dominate everything you put your hands to, you leave your inheritance on the table. Don't make the same mistakes the children of Israel made. Don't make the same mistake the saints that came before us made. Assume your position!!!

Chapter 5

You Are Called to Entrepreneurship

Now that you understand you have been positioned within the Earth to establish order and bring answers to those you are purposed to help, let's discuss the call of entrepreneurship. Like any other call, it is a unique mantle given to specific individuals God has equipped for the journey. It is not simply owning your own business. It is a weighty designation by the Creator for the children to whom He has given special gifts. It is not to be taken lightly, or as just another business to buy into. This call should be weighed with the same weight of ministering in any other way. If you wouldn't run and start a church just because you felt like it, you shouldn't start a business that way either.

The bible teaches us that the steps of a good man are ordered by the Lord, and He delights in his way. (Psalm 37:23). I'm going to do a little theological bible study with you but stick with me. As the preachers would say... I promise it'll bless you! According to Strong's Complete Dictionary of Bible words, the word step here is derived from the Hebrew word, mits`ad, which means a step, or goings. With that in mind, the goings of a good man are ordered by the Lord, and He delights in his way. Simple, right? Let's continue…the word order in this verse was transliterated from the Hebrew term kuwn, which means to set firm; to establish. The goings of a good man are firmly established by the Lord, and He delights in his way. The one who delights in this verse is Jehovah, the one true God. Jehovah himself takes pleasure in the way of a good man. The final word in this verse comes from the Hebrew term derek, which means road; distance; journey; manner. Catch the significance of what this verse is saying. The goings of a good man are firmly established by Jehovah, and He (Jehovah) takes pleasure in his (the good man's) journey! The Lord not only sets us on the path of entrepreneurship by firmly establishing our goings, but He takes pleasure in the JOURNEY! Let that sink in for a moment. God, the creator of the entire universe is not only concerned about what I do with this life He has given me, but He establishes a path for me that brings Him pleasure. I believe the journey brings God pleasure because it is the shaping process which brings us into proper alignment with Him. He doesn't take pleasure in our suffering or struggles, but it delights Him to see His children growing. Just as a human father experiences joy as he watches his children grow and experience new things, so does our Heavenly Father. Why would I ever despise what brings my Father pleasure? I can't despise the difficulty of the journey if I say I want God to be pleased with my life. I can't accept the good and reject the bad. I must understand that the trying of my faith produces patience and allow patience to have her perfect work so that I can be perfect and complete, lacking nothing. (James 1:3-4) The journey, everything that transpires as we endeavor to answer the call to entrepreneurship, is God's opportunity to smile upon His children as we grow into the vessels of honor He created us to be.

We are established in the journey!

When I think about being firmly established, I think about how God established everything else in the Earth. He spoke to the Earth and said, "let there be light". He never said, let's create a sun, moon, or stars. No… He spoke light and the universe intuitively knew what needed to be formed in order to obey the command of the Creator! When the Lord saw that the light was good, He affirmed and sustained it! (Genesis 1:3) Every form of creation has the ability to intuitively respond to the voice of God, and therefore be firmly established by Him. You were never expected to begin the path of entrepreneurship alone. You were called to respond to the voice of God, which will firmly establish, affirm, and sustain you all the days of your life. In all the years of the Earth, the sun has never stopped responding to "let there be light". It's never been confused about where it was supposed to shine. It rises and sets at exactly the right moment to give way for the moon and stars to obey their portion of the command. Each one understands they have a God-given mandate to follow in order to obey His command. The same is true for the ocean, land,

and sea. The moment God said, "let the waters under the heaven be gathered together unto one place and let the dry land appear," the Earth responded, and it was so. (Genesis 1:9) From that moment to this one, the ocean has never forgotten its borders. Even through horrific natural disasters, the ocean doesn't forget it's coordinated. The wind pushes the ocean and causes great disruption, but as soon as the wind calms, the ocean rests in the exact place God ordained for it to occupy. From the days of creation until now, a seed has never stopped producing after its own kind. Apple trees didn't decide to start producing oranges. Nature does what it was created to do without God having to remind it of the order He established. Man is the only form of creation that consistently requires a reminder of His command.

Instead of intuitively responding to God's command, man has become influenced by the thoughts and suggestions presented by the enemy just as Eve did in the garden. (Genesis 3:4-5) Anyone who has walked with God any length of time and has read the bible knows we were created to have dominion. Yet, when God calls us to entrepreneurship, instead of learning how to access that dominion, we listen to the suggestion that maybe we heard God wrong. Maybe we misunderstood. Maybe the timing just isn't right because the economy isn't where it needs to be. We accept all of those suggestions as though God was unaware of the state of the economy before He issued the call. Instead of casting down imaginations, and every high thing that exalteth itself against the knowledge of God, and bringing into captivity every thought to the obedience of Christ (2 Corinthians 10:5),

Goodbye Egypt

we accept the thoughts as legitimate reasons we should hold off on acknowledging our call. When we accept those thoughts and legitimize them in our minds, we allow the enemy to impede God's process of establishment. That is literally the enemy's oldest trick. He introduces the idea that maybe what God said wasn't true, and if that doesn't work he circles back with, "Maybe that word wasn't for you." He throws around terms like practical and common sense. He weaves the lie in with the truth and appeals to your natural mind. Following God and answering His call is not about your natural mind or what makes sense here in the Earth realm. It is all about believing God and trusting Him even when the situation looks impossible! True faith is continuing on God's path for your life even though natural circumstances urge you to quit.

There will always be natural reasons that seem to justify you working a traditional 9-5. No matter how strong our connection to God is, there are risks associated with being an entrepreneur. Working for someone else means they assume the risk. However, it also means they reap the benefits of that risk while leveraging your skills and work ethic to achieve their goals. They are accepting their call while you're ignoring yours. While they may be providing a steady paycheck for you, deep down inside you know you aren't doing what you were created to do. Intuitively you know what God has called you to. You feel the discontentment that is simmering deep within you. Your mind may be tricked into believing the lies of the enemy, but your spirit knows the truth. Just like every other form of creation, your spirit knows how to produce that which God has spoken. When you allow your mind to come into agreement with your spirit, everything you've been praying for will manifest. God's decree over your life is success. Your mind may not know exactly how to get there, but just as the universe understood it needed to produce a sun, moon, and stars to obey God's command for light, your spirit knows exactly what it needs to produce to obey God's command for dominion! You must learn to listen to your spirit, not your mind.

<u>Very Good!</u>

Genesis 1:26-31 -And God said, Let us make man in our image, after our likeness: and let them have dominion over the fish of the sea, and over the fowl of the air, and over the cattle, and over all the earth, and over every creeping thing that creepeth upon the earth. So God created man in his own image, in the image of God created he him; male and female created he them. And God blessed them, and God said unto them, Be fruitful, and multiply, and replenish the earth, and subdue it: and have dominion over the fish of the sea, and over the fowl of the air, and over every living thing that moveth upon the earth. And God said, Behold, I have given you every herb bearing seed, which is upon the face of all the earth, and every tree, in the which is the fruit of a tree yielding seed; to you, it shall be for meat. And to every beast of the earth, and to every fowl of the air, and to every thing that creepeth upon the earth, wherein there is life, I have given every green herb

for meat: and it was so. And God saw everything that he had made, and, behold, it was very good. And the evening and the morning were the sixth day.

Man is the only form of creation God touched and breathed HIS breath into. This is how we know we are His highest form of creation.

Throughout the story of creation, God routinely reflected upon His work at the end of the day. He reviewed His progress, saw that it was good, and concluded the day. The statement "and God saw that it was good" is frequently recorded prior to God calling an end to the day. However, on the day God created man, it went beyond a simple "it was good". On the day man was created, when God examined all His work, He saw that it wasn't just good, it was ***VERY*** good. God has always taken extra care with man. Man is the only form of creation God touched and breathed HIS breath into. This is how we know we are His highest form of creation… because we are the only form created in His image and likeness and the only one He didn't just speak into existence. He took His time and fashioned man from the dirt. He was powerful enough to speak life into man, but God chose to breathe life into him. The significance of this decision is a demonstration of God's love for man, and His intentionality towards our lives. Even with all the care God has shown towards man, we're still the only form that has the ability to doubt Him. He could have created us to be slaves to Him, unable to choose our own path, but He desires that we return His affections willingly, so He gave man free will. That will have often landed man in hot water because we don't always choose wisely, but it also adds value to our obedience. We aren't obedient because we are forced to do so. We are obedient because we choose to serve God and endeavor to keep His commandments. We don't always get it right, but when your heart is to please God, He smiles upon your efforts. Despite what the enemy tries to make you believe, from the days of creation until now, you are approved! God looks upon you and declares, it is very good!

Just as God's eternal word towards man is, "it is very good", so should your word be concerning your daily work. God's example is set before us to reveal the structure of work. First, He created, then He reflected, and finally He rested. He spoke the result He desired to see. He didn't get bogged down on the details and speak to the details. Like I previously stated, He didn't speak to the sun, moon, and stars. He said, "let there be light," and there was. So often we get tricked into not declaring "let there be" because we keep trying to figure out "how it will be". You aren't called to determine "the how." As you move forward in your business and you feel the urge to launch a new product, service, or division, understand the key component to manifestation is to follow the example of your King. Issue the decree with the full understanding that the Earth realm is intuitive enough to produce that which you speak. It knows the details, even when you do not. The dominion that rests upon your life is recognized and respected in the Earth. The Earth was not given free will. It must do exactly as instructed. When you speak financial increase, it must produce everything required for that increase to hit your life and business.

Now you may be thinking, that all sounds great, but where is the work? Where do I add actions to my faith? When you issue the decree, that is the first action. Other than forming man, God didn't physically put His hands to work. We must kill the lie that we must work for ***everything***. You don't work to receive promises, you get into position to receive them. The physical work of growing your business is not what brings success. Yes, you must do the physical work, but that isn't what determines how successful you'll be. If it did, everyone who put in the same amount of work would have the same level of success. We all know that's not how things work.

What you do in the spirit causes things to manifest in the natural. It causes the right people to cross your path at the right time. It weaves that vacant building you've been driving by for years into a viable headquarters for your church or business. Have you ever really taken the time to think about the number of things that seemed to just fall into place at precisely the right time? That is the fruit of your obedience to God. It is the Earth producing that which is needed to obey your command. You didn't work 70 hours a week for that. You got into position and what was already decreed and won in the spirit manifested in the natural. That building was yours the moment God revealed it to you!

When it comes to the natural side of things, the day to day efforts of running your business, you only physically do what God directs you to do. That means if you decree, "let there be a flood of revenue for my store," you don't have to bog yourself down with busy work to make the decree manifest in the natural. Instead, stay in prayer and consult the Lord for direction. If He tells you to open your store for three hours a day, open your store for three hours a day. If He tells you to introduce new products, introduce new products. The works that accompany your faith are not the physically draining, long hours we have been tricked into believing we must put in to live in abundance. The works that accompany your faith are the instructions you receive directly from God! If you don't believe me, read Matthew 4:18.

Also, note that God made it a point to highlight to us that He rested on the 7th day. In this day of "the grind never sleeps" and internet comparison it can be easy to fall into the lie that you must work your fingers to the bone around the clock in order to be successful. That is a trick of the enemy to snatch man from his seat of authority. It's difficult to remember you have been given dominion over the Earth when you are exhausted from working seven days a week. Your business should be built around your lifestyle, not the other way around. We don't exist simply to make money. God has a life full of joy, mission, purpose, love, fun-filled experiences for us. When we step out of position and begin to try to work for everything instead of using our mouths to create that which we desire to see, we lose some of those moments. God showed us that He rested, not that He worked 10-

Goodbye Egypt

12 hours a day. That means rest is a heavenly principle, work is not.

God never intended for man to struggle. The manifestation doesn't come from you working your fingers to the bone. The manifestation comes from you following God's guidelines for creating and walking in total obedience to His word. Obedience not only opens doors, but every single act of obedience leads you directly to the door of opportunity. The doors of opportunities are created as the Earth realm obeys the decree you issued. Remember, you have dominion for a reason. Use it wisely and use it often!

Another reason many people are unable to acknowledge their personal call to entrepreneurship is that answering the call requires total faith in God to supply their needs. Well, scripture says my God shall supply all of my needs according to His riches in glory by Christ Jesus. (Philippians 4:19) We quote this scripture often, but when God calls us to stand on it, we waiver. Why would man, the one God gave special attention to, shrink back in doubt? Why do we choose to trust a corporation more than we trust God? Companies have been closing and laying people off for as long as they've been in existence, yet we'll trust them enough to stay with them during restructuring, waves of layoffs, store closures, etc. The moment God calls us to entrepreneurship and a dry financial season is experienced, we abandon the call and run back to Egypt. We allow the enemy to convince us the venture was not a call of God, but a simple idea we had that didn't work. We accept failure as the outcome, rather than going back to God and asking for strategies to make the company more financially successful. When your faith in God is unwavering, you'll understand that even though the Red Sea is before you, God has a prepared path. If He has to part the sea, He'll do so to ensure you reach your destination. Remember, God never calls us to a place He's unable to carry us through. He's never dropped one of His children. He's never forgotten to feed any of us.

Instead of viewing your business as another way to make money, understand God is far more intentional than that. From the very beginning of time, God ensured man was fully provided for. God intentionally created the dwelling place of man and placed what man would need to survive all throughout the Earth. The Lord fully established man's assignment before man was ever created. "Let us make man in our image, after our likeness: and let them have dominion…" Did you catch that? God established man before he created man! When you understand dominion is not just something for a few people, but it is God's decree over ALL, you'll readily acknowledge and accept your call to business and/or ministry. You were created in the image and likeness of an Establisher. That means not only am I capable of doing what He does, but I am also equipped to do so because He gave me His image and His likeness. I am to be a reflection of Him in the Earth, just as my children are reflections of me. God, our Father, has breathed Himself into us, His highest form of creation, the ones He sent His only begotten son to save! He thought so much of us that He went the extra mile to ensure we

Goodbye Egypt

were equipped and prepared. Walking away from what God has poured so much intentionality into is like a slap in His face! Why would you forfeit your right to establish?

Often, we view things from our head knowledge. We view situations as though they are isolated incidents. God is much more intentional than that. Romans 8:28 speaks about all things working together. This verse is often used to encourage individuals when they are facing tough times. I submit to you this verse goes so far beyond a tough season. All things work together… your job, your family, the church you attend, your passion, the business He prompted you to start, the good days, the dark nights… ALL of these things work together for your good! Your call to entrepreneurship is a part of God's strategic plan for your life. He's cultivating a mindset in you that is preparing you for the journey. He uses the "things" to teach us, mold us, and order our steps. He teaches us how to establish and be established. He walks with us, nudging us to trust Him more and build up our faith. He teaches us the Heavenly principle of rest. He reveals the keys to manifestation and dominion. He does all of this and more to equip us for the call of entrepreneurship.

If you've previously viewed your business as simply a revenue stream, I challenge you to lay that point of view before the Lord. Don't just take my word for it, but earnestly seek Him for a deeper revelation of His call on your life. You have been positioned in the Earth to be used by God. You must understand that every direction

He gives works to that end. This call is not about you and how business savvy you are or aren't. It isn't about keeping up with all of the fallacies presented on social media. It's not even about you manifesting your dreams. Your dreams are just another "thing" that is working together for your good. This journey that God takes pleasure in, is about you answering His call on your life, and how that call brings you into proper alignment with Him so that others will be blessed as a result of your obedience to Him. Whether you're launching a business, product line, or ministry, God is calling you back to Himself. If you view entrepreneurship as just another way for you to make money, how will you ever properly seek God for His guidance concerning your company? How can you reject the human workhorse mentality and embrace God's principle of rest? How can you learn to take pleasure in the journey just as God does? The answer is, you can't. You can't do any of those things without viewing your business from the right perspective. Your business or ministry launch is your human response to the call of God on your life! Accept and embrace your call!

Chapter 6

Learn the Power of Heavenly Strategies

When the Lord began dealing with me regarding the merging of faith and business, I didn't immediately understand how the two intertwined. I've owned multiple businesses over the years, all of them only having a measure of success. I hold a Bachelor of Science degree in Business Administration. I've successfully managed businesses for others and enjoyed it. On the other hand, I'm a woman of strong faith. I love God with everything in me, and I love serving His people. Since my teenage years, I've faithfully served the ministries I've attended. I've done everything from clean the church to teaching Sunday school, and even ministering on Sunday morning in the absence of my pastor. I would happily serve all day Sunday, then return to work on Monday in business professional mode, honestly believing the two would never meet.

Otescia R. Johnson

It wasn't until late 2017 when the Lord revealed to me His plan for my business, that I began to ask Him about the merging of the two worlds. I was a firm believer in keeping business separate from faith as to not exclude or isolate anyone, because it just didn't make sense to the business side of my brain. All I saw was a diminished market share which would potentially impact my bottom line. I believed speaking about God would be a turn off to nonbelievers. Their money is green. The wealth of the wicked is laid up for the just, right? I'd be crazy to undercut my own business by offending potential customers by talking about God all the time. It just didn't make sense to me.

Every business and marketing class I'd taken led me to that pattern of belief. Putting the potential revenue loss aside, my faith was my faith, and my business was business. Why would God have a plan for my business? What did the two even have to do with each other? It was those questions that prompted me to dig deeper with God. I wanted to see exactly what He was saying. I needed to understand. In the way that only He can, God led me to His word and showed me exactly how my faith and business were connected. He took me to the story of Jacob.

Jacob, who was a descendant of Abraham, was an heir to the promise of the seed of his grandfather. He preyed upon his brother's weakness to get it, but we'll get to that in a moment. After Isaac blessed Jacob, he provided his son with clear instructions as to where to go to find a wife. Jacob was told not to choose a wife from amongst the women of Canaan (Genesis 28:1), but to journey to

Goodbye Egypt

Padanaram and take a wife from the house of Laban. Jacob obeyed, and set out towards the city. It was during this journey that the pieces of his story began to make sense and the Lord confirmed Isaac's blessing over Jacob's life.

In Genesis 28: 12-15, the Lord visits Jacob by way of his dreams and provides a glimpse into the spirit realm. In the dream, the Lord revealed a ladder that reached all the way to heaven and the angels of the Lord were ascending and descending the ladder. At the top of the ladder stood the Lord as He issued a promise to Jacob.

"And, behold, the Lord stood above it, and said, I am the Lord God of Abraham thy father, and the God of Isaac: the land whereon thou liest, to thee will I give it, and to thy seed; And thy seed shall be as the dust of the earth, and thou shalt spread abroad to the west, and to the east, and to the north, and to the south: and in thee and in thy seed shall all the families of the earth be blessed. And, behold, I am with thee, and will keep thee in all places whither thou goest, and will bring thee again into this land; for I will not leave thee, until I have done that which I have spoken to thee of. - Genesis 28: 13-15

The significance of this moment and vision will be revealed in another chapter of Genesis, but what I want to first point out is that God is so concerned about your success that He will continually provide a vision for you to work towards. Jacob set out on the journey in search of a wife and to escape his brother Esau who'd issued a death threat against him. He was essentially running for his life, but God had a much larger plan.

So often we dismiss the danger zones of our lives as attacks from the enemy. We rarely consider the danger zone as an opportunity for God to move on our behalf. We don't slow down enough to see into our future. The vision God gave Jacob was important, but even more importantly, God spoke the word directly to Jacob. We know that faith cometh by hearing and hearing by the word of God. (Romans 10:17) When this verse was recorded, there was no bible. Therefore, the word of God they received in those days had to have been the spoken word. The Old Testament is full of accounts of God speaking directly to man. It is that heart to heart conversation with God that provides man with faith to believe God has already established a pathway of manifestation for everything He speaks or has spoken.

Your sin does not negate your call!

When we use those moments of, what feels like, intense attack to sit with God and hear His heart on the matter, we open ourselves up to receive far more than we even thought to ask for. Jacob could have every easily doubted he'd received the manifestation of the blessing because although his father spoke the blessing over him, he knew he'd done wrong. He preyed upon Esau's weakness and asked him to trade his birthright for food, **and** tricked Isaac into blessing him instead of Esau. Twice he'd wronged his brother, and we know he was unsure about what he'd done because in Genesis 27:12 he expressed

Goodbye Egypt

to his mother that he feared bringing a curse upon himself instead of a blessing.

That's exactly what we go through. When it's time for us to move into greater levels of blessings, rather than accepting the blessing is God's will for us, we begin to worry about all of our past sins. We stress out about our own worthiness as though God wasn't aware of what we'd do before we ever did it. Jacob's trickery and usurping of Esau was prophesied while Rebekah carried the twins in her womb. In Genesis 25:23, the Lord spoke to her and told her she was carrying two nations in her womb, one of which would be stronger than the other, and the elder would serve the younger. So, while it seemed everything Jacob did was wrong and sinful, his actions were fulfilling a prophesy the Lord had already revealed to their mother. Esau's wrath towards his brother pushed Jacob right into his destined place. The vision and the word God declared over him were the confirmation that although his method of getting there was unconventional, He was brought to the very place he was destined to occupy!

God has a strategy in place long before we are ever aware of the situation. By the times our minds can comprehend what is happening, we're right in the middle of God's strategic plan to bring us into our place of greatness. Much like Jacob started his journey to escape danger and find a wife, many kingdom entrepreneurs start businesses with simple goals in mind. We want to make more money and not have to work for anyone else. The truth of the matter is, God has been fashioning you for a Bethel (Genesis 25:19) experience since before you were conceived in your mother's womb. While you're looking for one thing, God is walking you directly to freedom! You may have thought this was just another business, but God is preparing you for marketplace ministry. While Jacob thought he was just going to rest before continuing his journey, that moment was the beginning of a whole new era of his life. God issued him a promise that would carry him through the next leg of his journey to freedom!

After Jacob arose and blessed the place he called Bethel, he continued until he reached a field full of flocks being watered by their caretakers. Jacob called out to them asking who they were and if they knew Laban. When the men replied they did, they also pointed out Rachel, Laban's daughter. When Jacob saw that Rachel was also bringing Laban's sheep to receive water, he rolled the stone away from the well to assist her. She in turn led him to her father's home. He resided with his uncle Laban, the brother of his mother Rebekah for one month before Laban mentioned Jacob working for him and asked Jacob what his wages should be. Jacob was already in love with Rachel, so he agreed to work for Laban for a period of seven years in exchange for her.

Now…let's recap. Jacob was fresh out of an encounter with God in which it was revealed that all the families of the Earth would be blessed through him and his seed. He has a great promise of possessing the land and having the Lord walk with him and keep him. Yet, he stands before Laban and says, I will work for you ***FOR FREE***

Goodbye Egypt

if you would just give me your daughter. Jacob is still thinking about his goal, which was to go to the house of Laban to find a wife.

When what the Lord says to you sounds so big that you can't even wrap your mind around it, it's easy to revert back to ***your*** original plan. Our human instinct is to overlook or reject the things that we can't imagine ourselves being able to accomplish. We tend to get stuck on the how by wrongfully assuming the responsibility of carrying out God's job of manifestation. We must remember, "how" it's going to manifest isn't our concern. God knows the how. Our job is to worship Him and keep the lines of communication open, so that we can obey every direction He provides. Those directions become the building blocks of God's strategy for success.

Jacob, still intent on carrying out his original plan, works for Laban faithfully for the full seven years. Laban then gives Jacob his daughter to marry. All seems well until Jacob realizes Laban has tricked him and given him Leah, Rachel's older sister. When Jacob realized Laban had tricked him, he confronted Laban who was unapologetic. Laban simply said, "It's only right that Leah be married off first. She's the oldest. Keep her and celebrate the wedding feast and afterwards I'll give you Rachel also. In return you will work for me for another seven years." (Genesis 29:26)

Jacob could have walked away, but his determination to marry the woman he wanted caused him to accept the offer. He stayed and continued to work for Laban. Over the course of time, Jacob began to have children with his wives and desired to leave Laban that he may establish a home for his family. However, Laban had prospered while Jacob worked for him. He wasn't willing to just allow Jacob to leave with his wives and children. So, Jacob made a proposal. He told Laban, "let me pass through your entire flock removing from it every speckled and spotted sheep and every dark or black one among the lambs and the spotted and speckled among the goats; and those shall be my wages." (Genesis 30:32)

What happens next, is a perfect example of how even our mistakes are a part of God's strategy for our success. Because Jacob sowed trickery, he reaped trickery. After making the agreement with Jacob, Laban secretly removed all of the male goats that were streaked and spotted and all the female goats that were speckled and spotted, every one with white on it, and all the dark ones among the sheep and put them in the care of his sons, (Genesis 30:35) Laban did this so that he could hold Jacob under his employment. He knew he'd done wrong, so he put three days distance between himself and Jacob. While Laban thought he was escaping to safety after trying to prevent Jacob from prospering, God revealed His strategy to Jacob, which created the revenue stream for Jacob's success.

"And Jacob took him rods of green poplar, and of the hazel and chesnut tree; and pilled white strakes in them, and made the white appear which was in the rods. And he set the rods which he had pilled before the flocks in the gutters in the watering troughs when the flocks came to drink, that they

should conceive when they came to drink. And the flocks conceived before the rods, and brought forth cattle ringstraked, speckled, and spotted. And Jacob did separate the lambs and set the faces of the flocks toward the ringstraked, and all the brown in the flock of Laban; and he put his own flocks by themselves, and put them not unto Laban's cattle. And it came to pass, whensoever the stronger cattle did conceive, that Jacob laid the rods before the eyes of the cattle in the gutters, that they might conceive among the rods. But when the cattle were feeble, he put them not in: so the feebler were Laban's, and the stronger Jacob's. And the man increased exceedingly, and had much cattle, and maidservants, and menservants, and camels, and asses." (Genesis 30:37-43)

Jacob's whole life led him to the place of God's strategy for his success. Even while in his mother's womb, the prophecy that was released spoke to his destiny. He tricked his father into giving him his brother's blessing. That trick sowed the seed of trickery that he reaped through Laban. Through Laban's trickery, God revealed a strategy to Jacob that allowed him to mate the animals in a way that caused all of the ones that were to be his to be strong. He far surpassed Laban's wealth simply by employing the strategy God gave to him. We know this was a God-given strategy because in the next chapter, Jacob reveals to his wives how he got the idea to mate the animals the way he did.

"And the Lord said unto Jacob, return unto the land of thy fathers, and to thy kindred; and I will be with thee. And Jacob sent and called Rachel and Leah to the field unto his flock, and said unto them, I see your father's countenance, that it is not toward me as before; but the God of my father hath been with me. And ye know that with all my power I have served your father. And your father hath deceived me, and changed my wages ten times; but God suffered him not to hurt me. If he said thus, The speckled shall be thy wages; then all the cattle bare speckled: and if he said thus, The ringstraked shall be thy hire; then bare all the cattle ringstraked. Thus God hath taken away the cattle of your father, and given them to me. And it came to pass at the time that the cattle conceived, that I lifted up mine eyes, and saw in a dream, and, behold, the rams which leaped upon the cattle were ringstraked, speckled, and grisled. And the angel of God spake unto me in a dream, saying, Jacob: And I said, Here am I. And he said, Lift up now thine eyes, and see, all the rams which leap upon the cattle are ringstraked, speckled, and grisled: for I have seen all that Laban doeth unto thee. *I am the God of Bethel*, where thou anointedst the pillar, and where thou vowedst a vow unto me: now arise, get thee out from this land, and return unto the land of thy kindred." (Genesis 31:3-13)**

The Lord revealed Himself as the God of Bethel. Remember that was where Jacob had the vision of the angels ascending and descending the ladder. God could have used any other point of reference to reveal Himself to Jacob, but I believe there was a specific purpose behind the reveal, a reason for God to make the connection between the occurrences. It is my belief that as the angels ascend and descend, they act as messengers between Heaven and Earth. They gather our petitions and take them to Heaven. When they return to Earth, they bring the answers, strategies, solutions, and manifested promises with them.

In the 10th chapter of the book of Daniel, an angel appeared to Daniel and confirmed God heard his prayer the day he spoke it. God dispatched the angel to bring the answer to Daniel, but he was held up by opposition and had to engage in war with the help of the warrior angel Michael in order to deliver the message to Daniel. Because of this reference and others that have been recorded, we know one of the jobs of angels is to bring answers to the prayers of man.

God, being full of intent and purposeful speech, made the connection because He was showing Jacob that He had prepared the answer for Jacob's solution back at the place called Bethel. God knew Laban was going to go back on his word just as He knew your boss would dangle a promotion over your head knowing full well the promotion would never come. God gave Jacob an encounter to prepare him for what was to come. If you notice in the passage of Genesis 31 that I have quoted, when Jacob spoke to his wives, he noted that God had been with him. Had God not revealed Himself at Bethel and then again when Laban was attempting to rob Jacob of his opportunity to earn, Jacob may have never had the faith to believe God was actually ordering his steps.

Your experiences with unjust employers and the knowledge of your own sin are motivators that push you to run to a quiet space alone with God. Out of those places, character is produced. Those moments caused Jacob who was formally a trickster, to walk in integrity and remain Laban's employee even after he knew Laban had wronged him. Had Jacob run off when he learned Laban had given him Leah instead of Rachel, he would have missed the opportunity to experience the power of Heaven's strategies.

There will be an hour to run out the door and never look back, but there are also times God will cause you to stay and serve in a place you know isn't your destiny. In due season, God will reveal the strategy that will not only provide for you and your family, but He will cause your wealth to out grow the wealth of the one who tried to hold you back!

As I mentioned at the beginning of this chapter, I've owned multiple businesses. I've leveraged earthly strategies in each, and I've also done the same for my previous employers. Like Jacob, everywhere I have worked, I have added success to the company. I was always a valuable contributor to the atmosphere and bottom line. I believed in working on my job as though I was working unto God, so I gave my best effort. I have always been rewarded with raises, bonuses, accolades, and even preferential treatment at times. Yet, like Jacob, I began to grow weary. I enjoyed helping others, but I longed to

Goodbye Egypt

build my own dreams. I began to pray and ask God to release me from traditional employment. I grew less and less tolerant of rules and systems that began to feel as though they were suffocating me. God was awakening me to His strategies for my future. Just as Jacob's whole life curated the strategy of God for his wealth, God was doing the same thing for me. Though I didn't initially understand how concerned God was about my success in business, He was strategizing to bring me to a place of supernatural manifestation of wealth. I also believe, He's doing the same thing for you. Everything you've experienced has been a part of God's strategy for your success. He has been slowly shaping and forming you. God used your mistakes, or things that seemed like mistakes, and turned them around for your good. (Romans 8:28).

Heavenly strategies are more than just good ideas you come up with in times of prayer. Heavenly strategies are powerful culminations of the order of God in your life. They free you to experience the overflowing abundance God created you to enjoy. God drops wisdom nuggets into us to equip us to activate the strategies of Heaven. The success you achieve through your own knowledge, strength and strategies, pale in comparison to what God has for you through His strategies. Yield your life and business to Him. Allow Him to lead you in the decision-making process, and when He reveals His strategy to you, don't hesitate! Move forward in full confidence in the ability of the Lord, your God, to perform exactly as He promised. It might sound crazy to expect animals to reproduce a certain way because of the way you feed them, but God has shown us through Jacob's story, that what seems foolish to man to confound the wise. (1 Corinthians 1:27)

Prayer for Divine Strategies: Father in the name of Jesus we give you praise, honor, and glory for the marvelous things you've done. We thank you for the Heavenly download you are depositing into us even now Lord, in the name of Jesus. God, we thank you for the manifestation of your word in our lives. We thank you for giving us dreams and visions of strategies that will take our lives and businesses to the next level. We take our place as your examples in the Earth for your glory. We give you praise in advance for the increased flow of finances that comes to us as a direct result of the strategies You give to us. We believe You at Your word and rejoice greatly, knowing You have already answered our prayer! In Jesus' name we pray, amen!

Chapter 7

Increasing Your Trust Walk:

Death to the Day Job

The journey of trust is one that will be ever unfolding before you as you walk with God. Just when you think you've mastered trust, God will call you to walk closer with Him, to hear His heart on matters that concern Him, to walk according to your spiritual eyes even when your natural senses tell you to run in the opposite direction.

For most children, the first scriptures they learn are John 3:16, the 23rd Psalm, or one of the many we pull out during the Easter season. Much like everything else in my life, my relationship with learning scripture was different. The first scripture I learned as a young person was Proverbs 3:5-6,

"Trust in the Lord with all thine heart; and lean not unto thine own understanding. In all thy ways acknowledge him, and he shall direct thy paths."

It took me years to understand this scripture was literally the foundation of my relationship with God. It is the scripture that centers me when I feel anxious about something God has called me to do. It is the starting point of every transition I experience with God.

In 2011, God began dealing with me about leaving the job I was working. I will never forget the day. I was driving from my office to a Christmas function. I was alone in the car, basically asking God to help me understand why I felt so unhappy and unfulfilled at work. I truly enjoyed the field I was working in, and my co-workers were decent people. I felt like I should be happy, yet I wasn't. Driving down the road that day trying and failing to hold back tears, I asked God, "What am I missing?" He responded, "Do you trust me?" I was shocked and blown away by His question. "Of course, I trust you Lord," I responded. I remember feeling exasperated as this wasn't the first time He'd asked me that question. Years prior He'd asked me to trust Him when it came to choosing the state my family would move to. I remember praying for God to reveal the home He had for us and Him replying that I hadn't asked Him what state to move to. I answered very quickly and honestly,

"God I am afraid to ask you where we should go. You might tell us to move to California or somewhere."

It took me about three days to get the courage to ask. When I did and He replied with North Carolina, I was slightly shocked, but knew my husband would be thrilled. I went straight to my husband and told him I believed God was directing us to North Carolina. Within

Goodbye Egypt

minutes my husband was on the computer and had found multiple homes in the area for us to choose from. Within a week we'd been approved to build a new home. Whereas, we'd been looking to rent a home in one state, trusting God and asking Him where to go, He blessed us to build our own home in the place He wanted us to live. In my mind, it was all perfect. I asked God the question even though I was unsure of how He'd respond. That seemed like trust to me. I told my husband what He said, and we'd obeyed Him without objection. Surely this meant I'd passed the trust test. I was wrong!

You see, every time God asked me to do something or spoke to me about making a move, I always gave Him a yes with conditions. Sure Lord, I'll preach your word, but please make sure my children are saved because I can't preach to everyone else and lose them. I acted as though God, in His infinite wisdom, didn't realize my own children needed salvation. I'd also negotiate my "yes".

"Yes Lord, I'll quit my job and start the business, but our bills must be paid, so I'll do it as soon as you replace the income of my full-time job."

I'd give God a yes that was half-hearted and laden with fear. Marry this man you've placed before me? Sure God, I'll do that but make sure He's worth it Lord. My heart can't handle another heartbreak.

Literally… every **yes** I'd ever given God had a "but" clause. I realized after going through some of the same cycles over and over again, that the key to success in my life and business required me to give God an eternal yes, one that did not come with a "but" clause or conditions God would have to meet for me to obey Him. To trust God is to obey Him without hesitation or objection because we are **SURE** He is faithful to complete every work He begins in us. When we drag our feet in yielding completely to Him, we often see doors begin to close in our face that force us to move in the direction God has ordained for us. For me, the door closed in 2013 when I was laid off from the job God started telling me to leave in 2011. He'd given me two years and I'd responded with but clause after but clause.

When I got the news of the layoff, I knew it was God pushing me in the direction He's been whispering about for years. I wasn't initially upset. I took it as a sign that God was going to cause all sorts of doors to open for me. I just knew I was going to start getting all sorts of invitations to preach all over the world. I saw myself writing New York Times bestsellers. I literally BELIEVED it was all going to happen overnight because of the years I'd spent serving God. In my mind, those years prepare me for the open doors. The problem with my thinking was that I assumed I was ready. I assumed my prayer life was strong enough to carry me into places I lacked the wisdom to navigate. That's NOT how God works. He will never send you to a place He hasn't prepared you for. The layoff was the beginning of my preparation season, which literally looked like everything I believed was a lie. Not only did the phone not ring with ministry invites, life got REALLY tough!

Goodbye Egypt

Four months after the layoff, tragedy struck, and my mother-in-law passed away. My husband had recently started a new job, but there was NO WAY we weren't going to travel to his hometown and stay there until the funeral. I watched my husband walk through the toughest week of his life knowing that when we got back home, he'd probably lose his job as well. The company wasn't heartless, but he was still in his 90-day probationary period and had taken 6 days off. From my professional experience, I knew he'd be released. I couldn't worry about that though, I needed to be present for him. After the funeral, my husband spent a little time visiting with family and friends before we started our journey home. The hour was late, and I knew he'd be too tired to go to work the following day, but again, I knew it was important for me to support him. God had been speaking to me the whole week about trusting Him. He'd reminded me multiple times that He'd never failed us in the past. So, I smiled and enjoyed watching my husband connect with people he hadn't seen in years.

Once we started the long 12-hour road trip home, the Lord gave my husband an open vision. I will never forget sitting in the passenger seat staring at him in awe, as he drove and revealed to me the open vision he was seeing. I was fascinated, but also knew God does not given vision without purpose. There was something coming behind the vision… something that would stretch our faith and test my confession of trust. As I sat there listening, the Lord began speaking to me as well. I could hear my husband and everything He was saying very clearly, but when He would pause, God would speak. I didn't tell my husband what was happening, I just listened to him. I didn't want to interrupt the flow. As His vision continued, he began to speak of the two of us traveling. At that point, I felt God nudging me to speak up.

I was hesitant, but I said to him, "Honey, I feel like the Lord is saying California." Instantly my husband chuckled and said, "I didn't want to say it because I know how you feel about California, but yes. We're going to go there."

I won't take you through all of the details that unfolded after that night, but a little less than two months later we were on the road MOVING to California! The Lord reminded me of our exchange a few years prior. I'd admitted that I was afraid of moving to California because I thought I would stick out like a sore thumb and be miserable. God challenged us to trust Him and go without objection. When we did, God showed up in more ways than I'll ever be able to explain in a single book. The move was yet another brick in the foundation of our trust walk. God used our time there to prove to us that He would always provide for us, even in the most expensive state in the country. We didn't realize it then, but God was strategically calling us to a higher level of trust that would become the backdrop for our entrepreneurship journey.

While living in California I accepted a contract assignment. Now, remember God had been speaking to me on and off for years regarding not working a traditional 9-5 job, but the pressures of bills and needing money to help provide for my family made me feel as though I had no

Goodbye Egypt

choice but to go to work. I accepted the assignment knowing it would be temporary. I was there strictly for a paycheck, and I absolutely HATED IT! The work was easy. I didn't mind what I was doing, but everything about the environment made me uncomfortable. I was assigned to a table, yes you read that correctly… a table, that was in the corner of an office shared by the lead recruiter and the HR Manager. They had their workload to handle, and I was given a laptop and phone at my table to handle mine. Both of those gentlemen were my superiors. They held meetings right there in the office. They made phone calls. They laughed and joked about whatever struck their fancy. All the while, I sat there at my table expected to be able to focus on my work and even call applicants with their banter in the background. Beyond that, neither of the men bothered to learn how to pronounce my name.

Now, please understand I am fully aware of the uniqueness of my name. I am not sensitive in the least when people see it and decide to call me Mrs. Johnson rather than attempting to pronounce it. On most of my previous jobs I was simply referred to as "O" and I am perfectly okay with that. I consider it a nickname. The difference was however, in previous times, my employer could actually pronounce my name and would gladly introduce me to clients without incident.

In this position, these gentlemen would stumble EACH time they said my name. I would smile graciously and pronounce it slowly. "O-t-c-uh" I'd say things like, "The E is long, or think of Alicia Silverstone, it's the same concept, except you replace the A-l with O-t." Being that we were living in Northern California, there were quite a few employees of Asian or Hispanic descent. Many of them also had names that are not common to the English language. I listened daily as every single one of their names were pronounced correctly. They could indeed correctly pronounce the famous actress' name. They took great care to pronounce other employees' names correctly. Remember I shared an office with them. I listened to them practice before hiring new employees. Yet, each time they needed to address me, they called me something different. It was usually one of three different pronunciations, none of which was remotely close to correct. Beyond that, there was no attempt to even simply refer to me as "O" as I suggested.

I would smile politely and try not to feel disrespected. I'd spent my life not making a fuss about my name. It's no one's fault my parents chose to be creative when they named me. I'm going into detail regarding this job because I want to point out, I made a real effort to be a part of the team. I worked to dismiss any idea of disrespect or feeling belittled. I'd smile and make small talk when addressed. I worked hard not to walk in the spirit of offense. At the end of the day, working there became more and more unbearable as the days crawled by and both men refused to make the effort. I worked on the tasks assigned to me, but my work was only acknowledged by the lead recruiter when the HR Manager wasn't in the office with us. The HR manager would only address the lead recruiter which was his right-hand man. Let me make sure you understand… I would do the work. I would submit the work. I would not be acknowledged. The lead recruiter would be credited for hiring candidates I recruited, contacted, pre-screened, and coached to interview for the positions.

One evening after a particularly difficult day I cried out to God for help in dealing with the difficulties at work. I asked Him why He would tell us to move to California only to send me to a job where they didn't care enough to learn how to pronounce my name correctly, or even acknowledge my contribution to the team.

God replied, "I didn't send you to that job. I told you to trust me."

I will not lie to you and tell you I instantly repented and left the position. I stayed there until the assignment ended and eventually went to work for a different company which wasn't great but was much more welcoming and accepting. Even in the new position though, I felt unfulfilled. This time there were no issues of disrespect. I knew the discontentment wasn't an issue with the job. I'd repeated my own mistake by placing myself in a job I should never have been working because of my inability to trust God to provide financially. I tricked myself into believing the way He was providing was through my job. I told myself the job with the great benefits was a blessing and I could not be picky about the way God chose to provide. I said all of those things to get through the workday, but the truth of the matter was when I spent time alone with God in prayer, He was consistently speaking to me about my writing. I was having dreams about characters whose stories were complex and diverse. I'd get up early to write before work, foolishly trying to convince myself that I was obeying God AND still holding down my day job. My actions were proof that I didn't trust God in every area of my life.

Trust in the Lord with all thine heart; and lean not unto thine own understanding. In all thy ways acknowledge him, and he shall direct thy paths...

"Paths? God, there's an 's' on path? God, is there more than one path?"

As I mentioned earlier, this scripture has been with me for as long as I have been aware of my need for God. I've NEVER noticed that path is actually paths! It's plural, meaning God is interested in every path I travel. He's concerned about the pathway I travel in my personal relationships, the pathway to my residence, the pathway of employment. These aren't all rolled into one big path known as the journey of my life. No, these are individual pathways I must surrender to Him for guidance. I'm not called to simply surrender to Him once. I am called to surrender every single path to Him, trusting that He will lead and guide me.

When I studied the word paths, I discovered one of the meanings of the term is: *"manner of life"* When I inquired of the Lord on this, He revealed to my heart, He desires to direct our manner of life. The way we "do life" is not to be guided by the standards of the world. We are taught very early in life to gain education so that we can

Goodbye Egypt

obtain a good paying job. As Kingdom citizens, we must surrender this thought process to Him. True, God's plan for some of His citizens may include traditional employment, but we must be careful not to assume that God's plan is one size fits all. Instead, we must surrender our manner of life to Him to discover His unique plan for us. This is particularly important for those of us who know we have been called to entrepreneurship.

After the difficult work experience, it took about three years for it to finally click that entrepreneurship was God's call for my life. It wasn't just something I was interested in or a fading desire. God had been preparing me to trust Him to lead me to the Promised Land… the place of destiny. I would never be able to access that place while holding on to the comforts of a day job.

The years spent wandering in the wilderness experienced by the children of Israel were intended to purge them of the thought patterns and belief systems of Egypt. It was a time to show them the provision and faithfulness of God before they entered into the Promised Land. It would have been a very short experience had they opened themselves up to the process. Instead, they complained and longed for the familiarity of Egypt, even though Egypt was a place of bondage. Truth be told, we do the exact same thing today. My willingness to stay on that job I described earlier, the job God never called me to, is no different than what the children of Israel did. I leaned on my own understanding, just as they did. I struggled to trust God in the face of what seemed like unsurmountable odds just as they did. How would they enter into a promised land when they had the red sea in front of them and Pharaoh behind them? How would I become a bestselling author with a family to feed and bills quickly mounting? How would I focus on writing when my stomach was rumbling? Why would I do that when I could go get a job that would quickly provide the money my family needed?

While we're are from different eras, the trust issues we experience as humans are the same. God desires to walk each of us from the place of bondage to the promised land, but to do so, we must trust Him completely. When I stopped living according to what I believed was best for me and surrendered to God's will for my life, I began to experience professional wins that once seemed implausible.

There is nothing wrong with having a day job IF that is God's plan for your life. When you KNOW you have been called to Kingdom Entrepreneurship, you must commit to trusting God even when things look like they aren't working for you. Trusting God always leads to a greater outcome than the one you envision for yourself. Don't become like the children of Israel wandering around in the wilderness, longing for the comforts of bondage (steady paycheck), when you are ordained to create more wealth than a job will ever provide. God has given us the power to get wealth so that He can establish His covenant with us, the covenant that was sworn to those who came before us. (Deuteronomy 8:18). Don't live your life ignoring that great benefit of your Christian life. He gave you the power so that you could use it to

Goodbye Egypt

accomplish the things He has placed before you. Your gifts are purposed to create revenue streams for you. Use them wisely. Instead of trusting the world's system which we already know to be corrupt, trust God, who will NEVER fail you!

Death to the Day Job Prayer: Father in the name of Jesus, we ask that you help us to remember the importance of trusting you in every area of our lives. Guide our decision-making process as we transition from trusting the system of the world, to being confident in the plan and process you have set before us. Lord, we thank you for reminding us that your resume with us is spotless. Help us in the moments that we feel pressed to remember this is all a part of transitioning from bondage to freedom and that every hard place is not a bad place. God, give us the wisdom and insight we need to purge our minds of the ways of the world, and show us the ways of the Kingdom. Help us to remember you are not man that you should lie, so every word you have spoken to us concerning our destiny is true. Give us the strength to continue walking towards the promise while you close the door to bondage. Introduce us to freedom in other areas of our lives so that we have a point of reference for freedom in our finances. Give us witty ideas and inventions that will shift the trajectory of our finances in Jesus' name, Amen!

Chapter 8

You are Called to Solve a Problem

One of the most difficult things for me once I committed to trusting God on this journey of entrepreneurship was understanding I wasn't called to business for the sake of being called to business. I knew everything God ordains has purpose attached to it, but I struggled trying to identify where my newly formed business fit in His plan.

What is the purpose that is attached to me being called to entrepreneurship?

When I sat before the Lord with this question on the table, He began to speak to me regarding things that come naturally to me. I've been called an optimist a time or two. I've had people say things like, "You just believe everything is going to work out." The truth is, I didn't always believe everything was going out, but I have always been the person who could see a way out of a sticky situation. I thought I was just a natural optimist, one who saw the glass as half full. After years of walking with the

Lord I understand Romans 8:28 is a pillar of my faith, but like everyone else, I still pray about situations that don't always look the way I think they should. The difference between me and most is that I seldom get sucked into depression when hard times come. I can often look at a situation and "see" a pathway to the end result we desire. I can believe that my plan will work because I am wired to see strategy. I don't see opposition as always being a bad thing. I can see how rough something looks and literally begin plotting a strategy to overcome the obstacle. While I have to surrender this ability so that I don't lean on my understanding, it is a gift that greatly helps me in business. It is the problem I am called to solve. My clients come to me with vague ideas and I am able to help them create a strategy to achieve their goals. This gift isn't something God gave me just to benefit my own life. There was a large gap in the marketplace my gift was intended to fill.

Before jumping full force into becoming a success coach, I went back to the Lord to ensure I was hearing Him correctly. I needed to be sure this wasn't something I'd come up with. My husband has told me many times over the years that people would pay me to teach them what I know. I heard him, but had difficulty believing it. My mother has told me since I was a young girl that people don't think the way I think. She's drilled into me that my mind is a gift. Still, I needed God to confirm this was the path HE ordained for me. I needed to know this was the manner of life He established for me, what He envisioned for me before He formed me in my mother's womb. To solidify this path, the Lord took me to Joseph,

Goodbye Egypt

son of Jacob. As you know, Joseph was favored by his father because he was the son of Rachel, Jacob's favorite wife, and he was born in his father's old age. Jacob openly favored Joseph causing his other sons to become jealous. As if that jealousy were not enough, God also favored Joseph and began giving him dreams. The dreams revealed that Joseph would one day be in a position of authority over his family members. Lacking wisdom due to his youth and inexperience, Joseph shared those dreams with his family. Not willing to serve their younger brother, Joseph's brothers threw him into a pit before he was taken away by the Midianites to be sold into slavery. (Genesis 37)

From the pit, Joseph was sold to Potiphar. While working for Potiphar, God once again favored Joseph and caused everything he did to prosper. Potiphar promoted Joseph to the position of overseer. While working faithfully in his new position, Joseph was propositioned by Potiphar's wife. Being a man of morals, he denied her advances. As an act of revenge for his rejection, Potiphar's wife lied and accused Joseph of trying to attack her. Romans 8:28, though it wasn't even written yet, comes alive in Joseph's life during this particular season. While in jail, Joseph overheard two guards discussing dreams and interpreted both dreams. Two years later, Pharaoh had a dream, and no one was able to give him an interpretation. Because of what Joseph had done two years prior, he was called to Pharaoh to interpret the dream. Not only did Joseph interpret the years of plenty and years of famine that were coming upon the land, he provided Pharaoh with instructions to ensure Egypt would be well taken care of during the famine. Impressed by Joseph's discretion, wisdom, and relationship with God, Pharaoh not only released him from prison, but he appointed Joseph over the land of Egypt. He made Joseph the second in command, only slightly beneath himself. (Genesis 41:39-45)

I want to pause a moment and highlight a key point. Joseph was shown his future through a dream, but the path to that dream came by way of the pit, slavery, and false imprisonment. So often, we turn away from the path God has ordained for us because the journey to manifestation is difficult. It looks as though the business isn't working, so you give up. It looks as if all hope is lost, so you walk away. Joseph could have easily decided to never interpret a dream again after his own dream landed him in the pit. He could have chosen to sit in the seat of offense. Instead, he continued being who he was always created to be. Everywhere he went, though people consistently tried to harm him, Joseph served proudly. He knew he'd been shown the dream of his family bowing to him, yet he continued to serve.

The path to ruling is often right through the position of servanthood and the trying of your faith. Can you still believe your dream will come to pass when you are falsely accused? Can you continue on the path of entrepreneurship when your very existence causes you to lose everything and those you love the most? Joseph went directly from prison to ruling over an entire country! I can imagine he had some dark moments while he sat wrongfully accused. There was no "story of Joseph" to encourage him. He didn't have the bible at his fingertips like we do. Yet, he held on until he saw the salvation of the Lord! He saw the manifestation of his dream by way of the darkest hour of his life.

I want to encourage those of you who are currently walking through your darkest hours. I want you to know the Father is not a man that He should lie nor is He the son of man that He should repent. (Numbers 23:19) Had Joseph's brothers never become jealous of him, had they never thrown him into the pit, had Potiphar's wife never lied on him… there would be no manifestation of his dream! He would have never even been in Egypt in the first place. He would have still been in his father's house experiencing only a small portion of what God had ordained for his life! The dark times he walked through put him in position to recognize the problem he was called to solve!

Joseph didn't solve the problem of managing Egypt's resources during the famine because he spent years going to school to study management. He didn't get promoted because he jumped up and down to get Potiphar's attention. He wasn't elevated by Pharaoh because he maneuvered his way into visibility. All Joseph did was walk uprightly before God! He didn't give way to bitterness or become puffed up when he received favor from man. Joseph remained faithful to God, and God being the faithful Father that He is, showed Himself strong on Joseph's behalf!

God stepped in at the appropriate time, just before the problem manifested in Egypt and revealed Joseph as the answer. Though Egypt had a ruler who was born to occupy that position, Pharaoh lacked the wisdom to interpret the dream AND provide a strategy because that was not his purpose in the Earth. His purpose was to recognize the solution in Joseph's belly and act accordingly. As a Kingdom Entrepreneur, there are a select group of people whose lives depend on you walking in the fullness of who God created you to be. They are waiting for you to reveal the answer they have been praying for… even if they don't know it yet.

When famine struck the land, Joseph's brothers, the ones who initially wanted to kill him, were forced to come back to him in search of food. They didn't realize the one they got rid of was the one who would ensure they had food to eat. Those you are called to won't always recognize you right away. Don't become frustrated and wash your hands of them. Instead, recognize that at the appropriate time God will reveal to them that the answer they need is in your belly. Like Joseph, you don't have to try to prove who you are or force people to believe in your dream. Your very presence becomes the revelation of the value you hold as you submit yourself to the call of God and follow the leading of the Holy Spirit!

When you are sure of the problem you are called to solve, your whole perspective changes when you run into difficult times. Rather than shrink back in fear, you hold your head high knowing the opposition is just coming to try to stop you from fulfilling your purpose. As I mentioned, I know my ability to see strategy where everyone else sees a roadblock is a gift from God. Like Joseph, I

Goodbye Egypt

have seen the hand of God on my life since I was very young. I knew I was created for something great, even when those who were older than me singled me out and attempted to prevent me from fulfilling the purpose of God on my life. My confidence in God's ability to make sense of the story of my life never wavered.

I was born as an answer to a need in the Earth, and so were you!

While I have not been thrown into prison because of my commitment to walking uprightly before the Lord, I have experienced financial difficulty, loss of relationship, self-doubt, and more. However, while thinking I was praying to overcome those things, God took me all the way back to the basics. He helped me to shift my focus from what I was experiencing to what I was growing into. Instead of crying over the hard days, I began to focus on problem solving and strategizing as God revealed new pieces of the puzzle to me. Before long, God had given me strategies to build businesses in multiple industries, teach business owners how to bet on themselves, and merge business and faith. God used my own life to teach me the problem I was called to solve. I didn't go hunting for clients. I didn't start a huge marketing campaign. I began to walk in authenticity and testify of the goodness of our Savior and how my walk with Him birthed a business a never saw coming. As I shared my story with aspiring authors and entrepreneurs, many could identify with my struggles and requested to work with me. God used those initial interactions to show me how many Kingdom Entrepreneurs know they are called, but don't know who they are called to or what problem they are called to serve. This became a large part of my life's work, revealing to me that this was God's strategy all along… to bring me to the place of providing solutions to problems I didn't even realize existed.

Goodbye Egypt

Questions for You to Consider:

- What have you overcome that can help someone else?
- What problem are you called to solve for those you serve?
- How do your natural gifts make life better for those you encounter?

Prayer: Father we thank you for revealing the problem we are called to solve. Thank you for bringing us to the place of understanding that enables us to flow as you have designed. Give us divine insight to see our lives and businesses from your perspective. Show us our unique position within the marketplace that we may not only earn a living, but that we may also point others back to you. Shield our hearts from the pain of the dark days so that we do not become bitter or distracted by our experiences. Strengthen our inner man so that we can continue to move forward until the manifestation of your glory in our lives. Thank you for choosing us to be radical world changers in a land full of those who are lost. We thank you for the light of your word, and the truth of your calling. We surrender our will to you so that we may be used fully for your glory. In Jesus' mighty name we pray, amen!

Chapter 9

Know the Purpose Attached to Your Profits

I was 18 years old when God told me I was going to be wealthy. I wasn't praying about money or my future for that matter, yet God spoke to me concerning my financial destiny during a Friday night worship service, planting a seed that would take years to develop. You see, I was born into a family that was marked by poverty. Up until age 12, the most successful people I saw owned extremely modest homes in a town that had little more to offer than sewing and furniture plants. By the time my immediate family relocated to a larger city, the poverty mindset has been engrained into me. My ambition in life was to make enough money to pay my bills on time. Though I began to see others who lived a more established lifestyle, I couldn't imagine the same for myself. I literally couldn't see beyond living paycheck to paycheck, praying there would be enough left over to buy food and put gas in the car.

Meager beginnings and the corresponding limited mindset aside, I had no clue what I could ever do to become wealthy. I can sing a little, but I am not even close to talented enough to become a professional singer. I'm not athletic enough to become a professional athlete. I have zero interest in the stock market so I couldn't see myself investing my way to great wealth. In fact, I was really only interested in preaching and teaching God's word because that was the one thing people had always told me I was called to do. I'd been serious about my relationship with God for a little more than a year and I believed preaching the gospel was the most honorable thing I could do. The problem with that thinking was that I could not imagine how one could become wealthy just by preaching. The gospel is free… right?

As I grew older and progressed in my relationship with God, I began to understand that while I am called to share His word with others, He also had additional plans for me in the secular market. He had a professional career for me that had nothing to do with sharing the gospel. It took me roughly two years to accept I was hearing Him correctly and step out in faith. Once I did, I experienced financial success for the first time that was a direct result of my creative abilities. That success led me to full-time entrepreneurship and eventually paved the way for me to launch my current business.

Feeling as though something was still missing, I felt the urge to fast and spend time in prayer inquiring of the Lord regarding the purpose of the path He placed me on. I can't quite tell you why I felt so unsettled except to say, God wasn't finished unveiling my destiny to me and my spirit would not rest until I knew more. That time of fasting and prayer resulted in a prophetic encounter with the Lord. He began to speak to me regarding influence.

Influence- the capacity to have an effect on the character, development, or behavior of someone or something, or the effect itself.   (Meriam-Webster)

In this day and age, there is much talk about influencers, and their effect on the way goods and products are sold. For many businesses, the endorsement of a social influencer is the same as money in the bank. These people of great influence tell their followers to buy a particular product and websites crash because of the additional traffic. There was an entire television series based on the influence of Oprah. Her endorsement routinely takes companies from obscurity to millions of dollars in annual sales. Influencers with large numbers of Instagram followers are routinely paid obscenely large amounts of money to post a picture of themselves holding products. Companies pay top dollar to be mentioned by those the social media masses choose to follow. It is a huge responsibility, though many of the current social media influencers only use their influence to increase their own bottom line. They shy away from things that are deemed to hurt brands. Rarely do we see social media influencers encouraging their followers to turn back to Jesus, although they are in the greatest position to do so. Instead, followers are enticed by liquor, expensive cars, multi-million-dollar homes, and have dangerous elective surgery to enhance their bodies. While studying the social media accounts of influencers, I heard the question:

Otescia R. Johnson

"Do you not see your own ability to influence an entire generation for Jesus?"

I was taken aback. *Me? Influence? No one knows me. How will I influence a generation?*

The Lord began to teach me regarding the life of Jesus. The mission of Jesus in the Earth was to influence man to turn back to God. His death and resurrection created a pathway to salvation for us all, but His life left an eternal influence in the Earth. Even today, you and I are influenced as we study His life and teachings. Before the term "Social Influencer" was even a thing, Jesus walked the Earth influencing everyone He encountered. He is our greatest example. If Jesus was an influencer, and the bible tells us that we are to do even greater works than the ones He did while walking the Earth, what does that mean for us?

You are not merely here on the Earth to make money and die. You are not here to live your best life while ignoring the one who is suffering next to you. No, my dear fellow Kingdom Entrepreneur, God has a purpose for those profits that are stacking up in your bank account. Your wealth is simply a tool to get you a seat at the table. The world was never meant to influence the world. The church has always been intended to disrupt the status quo of a dying world by introducing Jesus to the culture.

[6] And this is God's plan: Both Gentiles and Jews who believe the Good News share equally in the riches inherited by God's children. Both are part of the same body, and both enjoy the promise of blessings

because they belong to Christ Jesus.[b] ⁷ By God's grace and mighty power, I have been given the privilege of serving him by spreading this Good News.

⁸ Though I am the least deserving of all God's people, he graciously gave me the privilege of telling the Gentiles about the endless treasures available to them in Christ. ⁹ I was chosen to explain to everyone[c] this mysterious plan that God, the Creator of all things, had kept secret from the beginning.

¹⁰ God's purpose in all this was to use the church to display his wisdom in its rich variety to all the unseen rulers and authorities in the heavenly places. ¹¹ This was his eternal plan, which he carried out through Christ Jesus our Lord. (Ephesians 3:6-11 NLT)

This passage nearly blew me away the first time I read it. It was confirmation of the words the Lord whispered to me during prayer. It was always God's plan for Jews and Gentiles alike to not only believe in Him and live according to His word, but to also share equally in the riches inherited by the children of God. We all belong to God, regardless of what we've done in our past, or the conditions to which we were born. We all enjoy the promise of His blessing and have the opportunity to be used by Him to tell the world of the benefits of a life lived in service to God. That was always a part of God's plan, even though He did not initially reveal it to us. He did not give us the power to get wealth just for the sake of getting wealth. (Deuteronomy 8:18) God is far more strategic than that. He knows the heart of man and exactly what it takes to draw man back to Him. Your position in the Earth, the success of your business, the visibility your platform affords you is purposed to lead others to Christ.

Success is attractive. No one watches a homeless man and thinks, man that is the life for me.

There are so many Christians who have accepted the lifestyle of poverty. I won't judge their choice, but it is very difficult to influence a generation to turn away from their lifestyles of self-indulgence and partying to convert to a lifestyle of poverty. Success is attractive. No one watches a homeless man and thinks, *man that is the life for me.* On the other hand, individuals who live in large homes and drive expensive cars are routinely questioned about what they do for a living. Strangers stop them to inquire. People admire them from afar. There have been television shows for decades that focus on the lifestyle of the wealthy. Millions of people become instant voyeurs hoping to gain some sort of insight as to what it would be like to live that way. Imagine if all of those wealthy people were kingdom citizens who told everyone the secret to their success was living a life led by the Holy Spirit. Can you imagine the number of people who would at least try to learn how to do the same?

Still not convinced? Have you ever been member of a church celebrities also attended? Have you ever noticed the number of people who will visit just to try to get a glimpse of the celebrity? Imagine if Michael Jackson were still alive and he announced he would be attending a particular church service on Sunday. Can you imagine the number of people who would stop everything to show up at that service? While they may have been going to see Michael, just their presence in the building would be an opportunity for them to hear the Good News!

This is the power of celebrity, wealth, and influence. I'm not suggesting every Kingdom Entrepreneur will be a multi-millionaire. Yet, we all have the ability to achieve the level of success God has ordained for our lives, and it is that success that paves the way for your influence. Your sphere of influence is valuable real estate and must be handled properly. When Kingdom Entrepreneurs begin to look identical to the world, we lose our ability to influence them for Jesus. We are intended to be relatable, not identical.

Your call to entrepreneurship and subsequently increased influence is so much bigger than you and your family. It goes beyond simply creating generational wealth for your bloodline. This is a vitally important piece of the puzzle of the great commission. In Matthew 28:19-20, Jesus appeared to the disciples after the resurrection and gave them clear instructions to go make disciples of all nations. We know the disciples did not have the transportation or communication mediums we do today, yet they were told to make disciples all over the world. How much greater do you think our mandate is given the technology and transportation resources we have available to us? With the push of a few buttons we can go live from any number of social platforms and tell the world about Jesus. The greater your success and influence, the more eyes will be glued to everything you release, putting you in the best position to fulfill the great commission.

To further solidify the purpose attached to our profits, let's examine Luke 5:1-11(KJV).

And it came to pass, that, as the people pressed upon him to hear the word of God, he stood by the lake of Gennesaret,

²And saw two ships standing by the lake: but the fishermen were gone out of them, and were washing their nets.

³And he entered into one of the ships, which was Simon's, and prayed him that he would thrust out a little from the land. And he sat down, and taught the people out of the ship.

⁴Now when he had left speaking, he said unto Simon, Launch out into the deep, and let down your nets for a draught.

⁵And Simon answering said unto him, Master, we have toiled all the night, and have taken nothing: nevertheless at thy word I will let down the net.

⁶And when they had this done, they inclosed a great multitude of fishes: and their net brake.

⁷And they beckoned unto their partners, which were in the other ship, that they should come and help them. And they came, and filled both the ships, so that they began to sink.

Goodbye Egypt

⁸ When Simon Peter saw it, he fell down at Jesus' knees, saying, Depart from me; for I am a sinful man, O Lord.

⁹ For he was astonished, and all that were with him, at the draught of the fishes which they had taken:

¹⁰ And so was also James, and John, the sons of Zebedee, which were partners with Simon. And Jesus said unto Simon, Fear not; from henceforth thou shalt catch men.

¹¹ And when they had brought their ships to land, they forsook all, and followed him.

Beginning at verse 1, we see that Jesus started the exchange between himself Simon Peter, James, and John with a crowd of witnesses. Jesus, knowing all, could have chosen a private opportunity to have this exchange, but as I just mentioned, Jesus uses your visibility as an opportunity to lead others back to God. Many Kingdom Entrepreneurs tend to avoid the spotlight because they do not enjoy having all eyes pointed in their direction. Being visible for God has nothing to do with us, but everything to do with what He is going to do next in your life! The eyes are watching the hand of God as He moves on your behalf! Remove the idea that the visibility is about you and embrace the fact that you are being blessed for His divine purpose!

When Jesus came upon the fishermen, they were washing their nets, which meant they were done fishing. Jesus, seeing an opportunity, sat in one of the boats and began teaching. I thoroughly believe this teaching was not only to satisfy the needs of those who'd crowded around

Jesus. This teaching was purposed to also build the faith of the fishermen. Before you can believe God for the abundance of overflow, you must spend time gleaning from Him. The time you spend in His presence encourages you and strengthens your faith. Faith comes by hearing, and hearing by the word of God. (Romans 10:17) Before you can trust God when He asks you to do the thing that seems implausible or impossible, you must have the revelation that comes from His teaching.

Immediately following His teaching, Jesus went to Simon Peter and gave him an instruction to go deep into the water and drop his nets. Keep in mind, this was Simon Peter's profession. It was his job to know how and when to catch fish. There was a reason they were washing their nets when Jesus originally approached them. They fished at night. They'd spent the whole night doing what they were trained to do and had no luck whatsoever. Now Jesus was telling them to do something that by ordinary understanding would not be successful at all. It went against their training to go fishing during the day. Yet, because they'd been taught by Jesus only minutes before, their faith was increased. Their capacity to receive God's blessing had been expanded. Therefore, Simon Peter agreed to do as instructed. Because they did what Jesus told them to do, not only did they catch fish, but they had to ask another boat to come help them haul in all of the fish they caught. Both boats were so full they began to sink. Simon Peter was so amazed at the large amount of fish they caught, he fell to his knees in front of Jesus. He knew it wasn't their fishing that caused all of those fish to come to them. It was the obedience to what Jesus had instructed them to do. He didn't try to take credit and pretend it was his savvy fishing skills that brought them to the place of abundance. He gave the credit to Jesus. Jesus then explained to them that they would become fishers of men.

So many people read this passage and get excited about the abundance of fish. I too, have read this and thought, "The blessing God has for me is going to completely transform our lives." While it is true, The entire experience was not about the abundance of fish. The blessing was a way to get their attention. The end goal was to make them fishers of men. Jesus approached the situation with a crowd of witnesses, not to bless the fishermen just for the sake of blessing them. He was strategic about who He blessed and who He allowed to see the blessing. We know this because there was a second boat of fishermen He could have chosen. We also know that the bible is full of instances where Jesus sent the multitudes away. This time He allowed people to remain as witnesses, and He chose the fishermen whose hearts He knew He could influence. Following the blessing, the fishermen did as expected and made the decision to follow Jesus.

You may have tried to make your business work over and over again. You may have taken every business course you could find and worked with every business coach you could scrape up enough money to afford, but true success won't come for you until you sit and learn from Jesus, then follow His instructions. It's okay to ask questions. We know it can be hard to accept that you're called to be a multi-millionaire who influences generations to come. Simon Peter knew what Jesus told him to do was a longshot, but he did it anyway. He didn't do it based on his own personal abilities. He did this because of the power on the inside of Jesus!

Here's a newsflash: What you are called to do IS impossible through your own strength, but when you submit to the teaching of the Father, you open the door for the abundance of blessings.

These blessings aren't solely for you. They are to increase the faith of the onlookers. They are purposed to bring you to a place of servanthood so that you too can apply those special gifts and talents you have to becoming a fisher of men. Your natural gifts are not coincidental. Your passion for the industry you occupy is not by happenstance. God knew exactly what He was putting inside of you when He formed you in your mother's womb. He knew my gift and passion for writing would be a useful tool to encourage people to turn back to Him. Your gift is intended to be used for the upbuilding of God's Kingdom. The success you achieve increases your visibility, your gift that paved the way for that success equips you to become a fisher of men. Your gift was always intended to point people back to God, the success just put you in position for more people to see you!

As you grow in clarity concerning your role and responsibility as a Kingdom Entrepreneur, you come into alignment with Heaven's purpose for your success. Your platform gives you greater visibility, thereby increasing your level of influence. Instead of the younger generation looking to athletes, actors, and performers for inspiration, they should be able to look at the lifestyles of Kingdom Citizens. There is a growing number of Kingdom Entrepreneurs who are speaking out about their love for Jesus, but we should not place that burden on a select few. Pastors of mega churches are expected to talk about Jesus. In essence, that is their job. What isn't immediately expected is to hear successful business owners telling the world to pray daily, read their bibles, and follow the leading of the Holy Spirit. We expect to see Christians feeding the homeless and caring for widows, but when is the last time we saw majority owners or CEOs of major Fortune 500 companies using their platforms to proclaim the goodness of Jesus as they launch initiatives that equip and empower the less fortunate? Rather than expecting secular companies to provide answers, it is our responsibility to be the hands and feet of Jesus in the Earth.

In our quest to reach the world we have to remember that God will use some of our businesses as vehicles of change. If you are called to start the next Amazon or Walmart, don't shy away from telling everyone how much you love Jesus. If you are invited to speak at a large secular convention or festival, ask the Lord how you can respect the rules of the stage while still introducing the audience to Him. If you are featured in Vogue, ask the Holy Spirit to give you a witty way to reference Him in your article. When we understand the purpose of our profits, we unlock the door for large scale witnessing. It's great that your private life is a personal witness for Him, but He also desires for your public persona to bring glory to Him. He anointed you for this stage, honor Him by leading others to Him.

Prayer for Influencers: Father, in the name of Jesus, we come to you humbly asking You to direct us as we move forward in business. Thank you for revealing to us the purpose attached to our blessings. Lord, we thank you for increasing our influence that we may be able to lead others to you. Show us how to consistently use this influence in a way that aligns with whatever is on Your heart. We submit our will to the throne and endeavor to please You Lord in all that we do. In Jesus' name, we give you all of the praise, honor, and glory, amen.

Daily Declaration for Influencers:

I decree and declare that I am wealthy and hold multiple positions of power and influence in the Earth realm.

I am the hands, feet, and mouthpiece of God, and it is my honor to point my followers back to the Lord.

I recognize the purpose attached to my profits and commit to using them wisely.

When I speak, change is released in the atmosphere and men and women are provoked to seek the face of God.

In all that I do, God is honored, glorified, and exalted.

When followers look at me, they see and recognize the work of the Lord.

I seek no personal glory but work to glorify my Father in Heaven who has chosen me to influence this generation.

I decree and declare that my business is successful and generates positive revenue daily.

My success attracts the attention of other influencers for the purpose of introducing a dying world to a living Savior.

I decree and declare that the words I speak are life and they go out to accomplish that which I have sent them to do. -Isaiah 55:11

Chapter 10

Assume Your Position:

Possess the Promised Land

Often when we come to this place in our journey, the place that comes after all the prayers, sleepless nights, sweat, hard work, and tears, we believe walking into the promised land is going to be a breeze. We believe the previous years of hard work or the time spent wandering in the wilderness is all that it will take to enter into the promise. I'm not quite sure where that thought process originated because the example set before us in scripture is the exact opposite.

In the 13th chapter of the book of Numbers, God spoke to Moses and told him to send spies into the land of Canaan. Moses did as God instructed, and the spies returned with fruit and the confirmation that the land did in fact flow with milk and honey. However, they also reported the land was already inhabited with giants. I think it's important to note God's direction in verse one.

"...Send the men to spy out the land of Canaan, which I am giving to the children of Israel..." (Numbers 13:1)

God is intentional with every word He speaks. The fact that He included the phrase, "which I am giving to the children of Israel," is a sign that there must have been a current owner or occupant of the land. If no one occupied the land, God would not need to "give" it to them. They could simply walk in and possess it. The coming events were more about God proving Himself to the children of Israel than the significance of the land or its inhabitants. The mere fact that God directed Moses to send the spies, also foreshadows things to come.

God always provides us with opportunities to trust Him and grow in our faith in His ability to perfect all things concerning us. This exercise of sending the spies ahead of time not only confirmed the land was as rich as God promised, but it was another opportunity for God to show Himself strong on behalf of the children of Israel.

Note to remember: God is always looking for an opportunity to bless His people. 2 Chronicles 16:9 KJV- "For the eyes of the Lord run to and fro throughout the whole earth, to shew himself strong in the behalf of them whose heart is perfect toward him..."

This is the same process we experience today in entrepreneurship. God has issued a promise to you that is even more amazing than He's revealed to you. Yet, there will still be obstacles you have to face as you assume your rightful position and possess the land. It is God's design for you to face hardships, as they present opportunities for Him to show Himself strong on your behalf. The opposition isn't about you or your destiny. It is a teachable moment for God to reveal another layer of His character to you.

Just as God led the children of Israel to a land that was inhabited by strong giants, (Numbers 13:31-33) God is leading you to a place that may already be occupied by individuals with larger platforms and more followers. You may look at yourself as insignificant compared to them, yet I want to point something out to you that will change the way you view yourself and your assignment. If you notice, the text never said the children of Israel were truly like grasshoppers compared to the inhabitants of the land. Instead the text states, **"And there we saw the giants, the sons of Anak, which come from giants: and we were in our own site as grasshoppers, and so we were in their sight." (Numbers 12:33 KJV)** The children of Israel saw _themselves_ as grasshoppers. They counted themselves as insignificant, just as many of us to today. God could have sent them to any other land, but I think He sent them to this particular land to prove to us that the promises He makes are not predicated upon the way we see ourselves or the way others see us. God makes promises based on the vision He has for our lives. It does not matter if there are "giants" in your industry occupying the space God has called you to. It doesn't matter if those giants ignore you because your small following does not seem like much to them. God's promise over you is sure! It won't fail.

Regardless of what others may think about you, it is your job to see yourself and your mission as a **Kingdom**

Entrepreneur through the light of the promise. Instead of falling apart and begging to return to bondage like the children of Israel (Numbers 14:1-4), take the position of Joshua and Caleb.

"And Joshua the son of Nun, and Caleb the son of Jephunneh, which were of them that searched the land, rent their clothes: And they spake unto all the company of the children of Israel, saying, The land, which we passed through to search it, is an exceeding good land. If the Lord delight in us, then he will bring us into this land, and give it us; a land which floweth with milk and honey. Only rebel not ye against the Lord, neither fear ye the people of the land; for they are bread for us: their defence is departed from them, and the Lord is with us: fear them not." (Numbers 14:6-9 KJV)

Joshua and Caleb saw the giants, but they understood a very valuable lesson, when God calls you to do something, He accompanies you as you obey Him. Instead of becoming frustrated with God when we face obstacles, we must assume the posture of Caleb and Joshua. We must not rebel against God and blame Him for the situations we face. The children of Israel were ready to forgo their promise, overthrow Moses as their leader, and return to slavery all because of a report of hardship.

The report of hardship is always worse than the actual hardship. It's how the enemy keeps you from facing the situation.

Goodbye Egypt

How many times have you wanted to throw in the towel because of fear of what was to come? How many times have you felt like you'd hit a roadblock so you must not be on the right track? How many times have you allowed your bank account to measure your success instead of trusting the process? I speak to entrepreneurs all the time who aren't making progress in their business because every time they see the giant, they become paralyzed by fear, instead of trusting the God that led them to the brink of the promise. I've spoken to individuals who make enough in their business to replace their 9-5 income but won't quit because of the giant of health insurance or retirement savings. They miss the fact that God already knew they'd need those things before He called them to leave Egypt. He is keenly aware of our needs and knows that if we'll just trust Him, the blessing of the promise will far outweigh anything Egypt has to offer.

Caleb and Joshua saw the giants. They knew exactly what they were facing, yet they had more faith than those who had only *heard* of the opponents. They were confident in God's ability to give them the land He'd promised to them. This is why God honored them and granted them access to Canaan while the others around them were not permitted to enter the promised land. (Numbers 14:30) Because of their complaining and lack of faith, the children of Israel, except for Joshua and Caleb, forfeited their right to the promise and died in the wilderness.

How many Saints have gone on to glory still living in poverty, even though God's word is clear regarding the promises He holds for His children? Did you watch your parents, grandparents, or even great-grandparents die with debt up to their ears? What type of witness is that for the future generations? How will we win the world for Jesus, if our own lifestyles do not reflect the attainment of the promises we say we believe?

As **Kingdom Entrepreneurs**, we have a unique call upon our lives to be the Joshua or Caleb of our day. We can see the same opposition everyone else sees, but our confession must be different. Instead of longing for the bondage of Egypt like so many around us, we must trust the God who literally holds the Earth together with His word. If all of creation is still standing by the word of God, how can we possibly believe His promises have somehow fallen to the ground?

God specializes in doing what seems impossible. His name gets the most glory when He performs miracles, when what manifests in one's life is scientifically impossible. How will you see the manifestation of the promise if you never face a giant? The setback you experienced, the business that failed, the seemingly insurmountable odds are all opportunities for God to show Himself strong on your behalf. It's another opportunity for the underdog, the few in number, the least likely to succeed to come out on top in spite of heavy opposition. This, my fellow **Kingdom Entrepreneur,** is the character of God being revealed to us in real time relevance.

> *Ephesians 3:20 KJV- "Now unto him that is able to do exceeding abundantly above all that we ask or think, according to the power that worketh in us"*

I know you may be unsure of yourself and your ability to possess all that God has promised you. Doubt may creep up at the most inconvenient times and attempt to rob you of the promise. If you can't remember any of the other pearls of wisdom released in this book, I want you to remember this, it is not your responsibility to cause the promise to come to pass! God is the one who is able to do exceeding abundantly above all that we ask or think. So, you may not think you are prepared to possess the land. You may think your business is too small to become the next world leader in your industry. You may think you are only meant to impact your local city, but I want you to know the miracle begins where your ability ends. It's not up to you to make things happen. Your responsibility is to trust God as He leads you to the promise. Follow Him with radical obedience and His miraculous favor will cause your reputation to go before you. (Joshua 1:10 KJV) Those who once opposed you will begin to fear you because of the favor of God on your life. Radical obedience opens more doors than your abilities ever will.

God knew exactly what He was getting when He chose you. He knew your strengths and your weaknesses. He knew your insecurities and your pride. Yet, out of all of his children, He chose you for this assignment. He placed something special inside of you that can change a generation. Trust Him to lead you to your promise!

Every Joshua Needs a Caleb

Recently I was teaching the story of Joshua and Caleb during my 5am prayer session with my online community, and out of nowhere I heard myself say, "Every Joshua needs a Caleb". I must note I had no intention of saying that. I didn't know where it came from or even what it truly meant, but as soon as I said it, I knew Holy Spirit had just released a wisdom nugget into the Earth realm. It came out of my mouth, but I can assure you that did not come from Otescia. After prayer, I sat with the Lord as I always do. I pondered on the significance of what that phrase meant. Even today, as I prepared to edit this chapter to add this section, I wondered,

What does that look like? Why does one **NEED** *a Caleb?*

The Lord, in His infinite wisdom, responded to my internal questions with one of His own? Can you imagine how difficult it would have been to remain confident in faith if you were the ONLY one to return with a positive report? Remember, there were 12 spies sent into Canaan. 10 returned with a fearful report. Only Joshua and Caleb had the faith to believe God would still do as He promised.

Years ago, as I watched the National Geographic channel, I saw a pack of hyaenas attack a full-grown lion and tear it to shreds. They were able to do this because the lion wandered away from the safety of the pride. When you are with another person of faith, there is a level of protection because you are stronger together. Scripture even mentions the multiplication of strength that happens when like-minded individuals pair up. In Deuteronomy 32:30 the question is posed,

> *"How can one chase a thousand of them, and two people put ten thousand to flight, unless their rock had sold them, unless the Lord had given them up?"*

This passage is pointing out the implausibility of a single man chasing one thousand enemies away, or two men chasing away ten thousand. The only way for such an occurrence to happen is for the Lord to be on the side of the two. While this is important, I also want you to notice God's math in this text. If only one man chases one thousand enemies away, accordingly to our natural math, even with the Lord on their side, two men should only be able to chase away two thousand men. What God is revealing to us here is the multiplication of strength that happens when we partner with those of like faith. When you connect with a fellow Kingdom Entrepreneur, you gain a person with whom you can share your thoughts and ideas with. You have someone else to remind you of what God has said about your situation.

So often, entrepreneurship is viewed as a lone ranger sport. We see images of a person sitting alone at their desk. We hear the stories of working for several hours at a time with little human interaction. We are wrongly convinced that to become successful we must work harder than anyone else and that we are better off doing it alone. There's a whole term for it. It's called solopreneur, and quite frankly, it's hogwash! No one makes it to the next level doing everything themselves, and no one experiences the promised land without having someone else in their corner to help pray them through. Most of us have a team of "somebodies" in other areas of our lives, but we leave them out of the party when it comes to business. There is this fear that if you tell anyone else what you're doing, they may steal your idea.

While plagiarism is a very real thing, the fear of it is a trick of the enemy to keep you isolated so that he can scare you away from the promised land. Make no mistake, your ultimate opponent is not the person who occupies the space in your industry that you have been ordained to occupy. Truth be told, there are over seven billion people in the world… there's space for both of you in that seat, but that's another story for another book. My point here is that trying to get to where you are going without the support of another like-minded individual is never a good idea. I imagine the journey back to Moses was full of conversation between Caleb and Joshua. I imagine they traveled back in great expectation of what was to come. I can close my eyes and hear them testifying to the goodness of the Lord and prophesying of the great victory ahead. They were able to nurture each other's faith because they were both working towards a common goal based on a single promise from God.

This is the type of agreement the enemy would like to keep you from experiencing. No Caleb possesses the promised land without a Joshua and vice versa. Instead

Goodbye Egypt

of trying to build your business and reclaim the marketplace alone, ask God to reveal the covenant partners He ordained to walk with you on your journey. We are stronger when we work together.

Please note, I am not suggesting you add a partner to your business. Instead, partner with someone in prayer, fasting, and speaking the word of God over your life and business.

The Final Leg of the Journey

Now that you are on the brink of the promise, it is imperative that you shift your thinking from one of "working" to one of "positioning". The promises of God can never be earned; therefore, we cannot work our way into the promised land. Accessing the promise requires two things: radical faith and radical obedience.

If you review all the biblical stories I've shared throughout this book, you'll find radical faith and obedience in each one. God is not looking for more workers. He's not looking for the person who can run the fastest, work the most hours, or pitch to the highest number of people. God is searching the entire Earth for those whose hearts are loyal to Him so that He may show Himself strong on their behalf. (2 Chronicles 16:9) The scripture never tells us God is looking for workhorses. He's looking for a people who will be faithful to Him and what He asks them to do. Your key to accessing this next phase of life and business is connected to your obedience to God's instructions. God requires strict adherence to the words He speaks.

If you examine the life of Moses, you'll find a man who followed God despite his own insecurities and short comings. He did great exploits for God and communed with God in a way that is seldomly recorded. Moses' life is a blueprint for experiencing the promise. Yet, in all his good works Moses still died before accessing the promise. Why? Because he did not follow God's specific instructions.

In the 17th chapter of Exodus, the children of Israel chided with Moses because they were thirsty and wanted water to drink. Moses rebuked them for tempting the Lord, but the Lord provided Moses with instructions to smite the rock and water would flow from it for the people to drink. Moses did exactly as God instructed him to do, and all was well. By the time we get to Numbers chapter 20, the people are complaining about water again. Moses, having spent years leading the people and allowing God to perform works through him, has now grown weary with the people. In this instance, God gives Moses instruction to speak to the rock and it will flow with water for the people.

Instead of Moses following God's instruction with radical obedience, he chose to rely on what He believed would work. He used an old method, (striking the rock) to produce the water, instead of trusting God's instruction and doing a new thing (speaking to the rock). He even went a step further and rebuked the people.

Goodbye Egypt

"And Moses and Aaron gathered the congregation together before the rock, and he said unto them, Hear now, ye rebels; must we fetch you water out of this rock?

And Moses lifted up his hand, and with his rod he smote the rock twice: and the water came out abundantly, and the congregation drank, and their beasts also." – Numbers 20:10-11 KJV

Moses' reference to the people as rebels reveals to us the frustration he felt towards them. His frustration was warranted by most people's standards, but God has a different set of standards. He requires faith and obedience regardless of what you may be feeling at the moment. God dealt swiftly and severely with Moses after his disobedience.

"And the Lord spake unto Moses and Aaron, Because ye believed me not, to sanctify me in the eyes of the children of Israel, therefore ye shall not bring this congregation into the land which I have given them." – Numbers 20:12 KJV

All of your previous obedience and faith does not secure your access to the promise. Each act of obedience brings you one step closer to receiving everything God has promised to bless you with, hence the term positioning. Your obedience puts you in the position to receive the promise. Moses was unable to shift from working (hitting the rock), to being in position to receive (speaking to the rock). His inability to follow God's instruction to the letter, resulted in him forfeiting all he'd worked to enjoy.

I've heard many people say Moses received a harsh punishment for his disobedience, but I disagree. While God is a merciful God, He must deal with those of us who have been called to a level of visibility differently. Remember, the 12 spies who were sent into the land of Canaan were all leaders in their tribes. Their words held weight in the hearts of those who followed them. Their bad report caused an entire generation of people to falter and ultimately die in the wilderness. Because of the magnitude of the call and the large number of lives who hold your words in high esteem, you cannot have the luxury of small faith or disobedience. If Moses would have been walking in radical faith, he would have spoken to the rock knowing that God was powerful enough to cause water to gush from it.

As you assume your position as a **Kingdom Entrepreneur,** there will be times when you will be tempted to revert back to old methods that have worked for you in the past. You will be tempted to make variations to the instructions God gives you. There will be moments of doubt as it pertains to the destiny God has ordained for you. In the face of it all, you must remain radical in your faith and obedience. You are held to a higher standard because of your call to teach and lead others. (James 3:1) You cannot afford to be tripped up by frustrations and other emotional strongholds. You do not have time to lament over how long and tedious your journey has been. Your window for those things has closed. Now, it is imperative that you assume the position to receive this promise that you have worked to obtain. Every act of faith has deepened your relationship with God. Every act of obedience has brought you one step closer to the promise. Now that you are knocking on the door of the promised land, do not allow circumstances, people, disappointments and the like to cheat you out of what was destined for you before the foundation of the world.

The world is in dire need of the influence that lies within you. Your ideas, inventions, systems, and tools have the capacity to change the way goods and services are exchanged globally. The desires you have to create change in the Earth were given to you by God so that as you commit your ways to Him and trust also in Him, He shall bring it to pass. (Psalm 37:4-5)

It is God's desire to use you to reclaim the marketplace so that you can influence a dying world to turn back to Him. You are on the brink of something that has never been done by anyone in your bloodline. Stay focused on hearing God and responding accordingly to what He instructs you to do. Learn from the mistakes Moses made so that you can enter into the promised land and enjoy the fruits of your lifestyle of radical faith and obedience.

Prayer for Kingdom Entrepreneurs: Father, in the name of Jesus, I pray for every Kingdom Entrepreneur who has read this book. I pray that You would guide and direct each step they take and lead them as they leap into territories unknown. Father, we trust that You see much further than we do and that You will speak to us at every critical moment directing us when to turn, when to keep straight, and when to sit and wait for further instructions. Help us to be comfortable standing out in a world that tries to force us to fit in. Thank you, Lord, for choosing us to be Your Kingdom Entrepreneurs who lead from the front by your example. Give us the wisdom and faith we need for this next leg of the journey. Help us to keep our eyes set on you even when the giants try to yell to get our attention. Increase our visibility in the spirit realm so that we see only what You desire for us to see. Father, tug on our hearts daily so that we may remember this journey is not about achieving worldly success and storing up riches, but it is ultimately about building Your Kingdom and leading others to enter into true relationship with You. We trust You Lord, to not only bring us to the point of delivery, but to establish us as Your thought leaders, innovators, inventors, and influencers within the Earth. We are Your Kingdom Entrepreneurs, and we humbly commit ourselves to serving You forever. In Jesus' name, amen.

About the Author

Otescia R. Johnson is a skilled writer, ordained prophetess, captivating and innovative speaker, published author, and mentor. Born in a tiny town in South Carolina, Otescia has always dreamed of a life full of travel and philanthropy. Even as a young girl she "practiced" helping people by "counseling" her dolls. As she grew older, she began to move towards business and entrepreneurship, two areas in which she excelled greatly. She studied Business Administration at Stevens-Henager College where she earned her Bachelor of Science degree. While she made a name for herself within her respective field of business, she found herself unfulfilled as her desire to help individuals overcome past difficulties began to consume her thoughts.

Otescia's desire to help people all over the world through her ministry materialized in January 2009 when she began to lead the Women of Virtue Ministry at the Grafenwoehr Christian Fellowship located in Grafenwoehr, Germany under the leadership of Pastor James Fleming. In addition to the Women of Virtue, Otescia opened her home weekly and facilitated group sessions aimed at providing a safe place for women to be spiritually vulnerable.

In 2012, Otescia took her home-based sessions a step further and founded O. Johnson Ministries, an effort aimed at equipping the whole woman to walk in the fullness of her purpose! She then launched the "Healing the Hurt" conference, which speaks to the broken places women often try to hide. In addition to managing O.

Otescia R. Johnson

Johnson Ministries, Otescia is the founder of B.O.Y. (Bet on Yourself) Enterprises, Inc., a corporation that helps believers merge their faith and business as they navigate the world of entrepreneurship. She is also the bestselling author of 12 published books, as well as the creator of the *Magnetize Your Life* and *Roadmap to Publication* systems.

Otescia is a firm believer in the sanctity of marriage and enjoys being married to her best friend and biggest supporter, Lyndell Johnson. Lyndell and Otescia met in an unorthodox way that led them to live by the phrase, "God has a way of doing things so that it can't be mistaken as anyone else". They quickly fell in love and have devoted their lives to each other and their six children. They currently reside in North Carolina.

Connect with Otescia

To connect with Otescia, you may visit her website: www.otesciajohnson.com to join her mailing list.

You may also follow her on Social Media:

Facebook: www.facebook.com/AuthorORJohnson

Instagram: www.instagram.com/o.r.johnson

To have Otescia speak at your next event, please direct your inquiry to bookings@ojohnsonministries.com

www.ingramcontent.com/pod-product-compliance
Lightning Source LLC
LaVergne TN
LVHW041627070426
835507LV00008B/493